Building Bridges through Sensory Integration

2nd Edition

Ellen Yack, B.Sc., M.Ed., O.T.

Shirley Sutton, B.Sc., O.T.

Paula Aquilla, B.Sc., O.T.

Las Vegas

2nd edition published in the United States by

Sensory Resources LLC
2200 E. Patrick Lane, Suite 3A
Las Vegas, NV 89119
Tel. 888-357-5867
Fax: 702-891-8899
email: Orders@SensoryResources.com
www.SensoryResources.com

ISBN 1-931615-12-8   Orginally published under ISBN 0-9685375-0-2

Dedication

This book is dedicated to the children and families with whom we had the privilege to work. They continue to inspire us, teach us, and challenge us. Your tenacity, courage, and strength of character are boundless.

Build Me a Bridge

I have known that you and I
have never been quite the same.
And I used to look up at the stars at night
and wonder which one was from where I came.
Because you seem to be part of another world
and I will never know what it's made of.
Unless you build me a bridge, build me a bridge,
build me a bridge out of love.

I long for the day that you smile at me
just because you realize
that there's a decent and intelligent person
buried deep in my kaleidoscope eyes.
For I have seen the way that people look at me
Though I have done nothing wrong.
Build me a bridge, build me a bridge,
And please don't take too long.

Living on the edge of fear.
Voices echo like thunder in my ear.
See me hiding every day.
I'm just waiting for the fear to lift away.

I want so much to be a part of your world.
I want so much to break through.
And all I need is to have a bridge,
a bridge built from me to you.
And I will be together with you forever,
and nothing can keep us apart.
If you build me a bridge, a tiny, little bridge
from my soul, down deep into your heart.

From Soon Will Come the Light: A View from Inside the Autism Puzzle by Thomas McKean. Future Education, Inc., Arlington, Texas, 1994. Reprinted with permission of the author and Future Horizons, Inc.

Contents

Letter to the Reader

We are continually inspired by the tenacity of children with autism and other forms of PDD. These children have been our teachers. Their efforts to participate in a world they sometimes find confusing have provided us with valuable information. As occupational therapists, we have also found the theory of sensory integration has given us a useful insight into the different behaviours these children can exhibit. We would like to share our experiences with you and help you to build bridges of greater understanding between yourself and the child with PDD.

To parents of children with special needs, this book is especially for you. It can be a tremendous challenge parenting a child with difficulties. It is our hope that this book will increase your understanding and provide you with strategies to help your child become more comfortable and independent at home. Also, it is our hope that this book will help you to strengthen your relationship with your child.

This book is also for childcare providers and educators. Inclusion is the hope of many parents and professionals who work with children with special needs. The unique learning style and behaviours of these children can be challenging in a classroom situation. The strategies provided in this book will assist you in creating a comfortable and safe environment, which promotes learning and social interaction.

We are very encouraged by the positive changes we have seen in the children we work with and the resulting changes in their families. This book outlines the theory and strategies we use in our practices. These strategies have been very successful for many families, and it is our hope that they are successful for you, too.

Acknowledgments

We thank our families for their support, and we also thank the parents of the children we work with, who provided valuable feedback during the preparation of this book. We thank Marg Whelan, Executive Director and Neil Walker, Program Director, of the Geneva Centre for Autism for their encouragement and assistance in the distribution of this book. Thanks to the Toronto Sensory Integration Study Group who believed in this project and provided a grant to assist in the publication of this book.

We also thank the following: Iris Greenspoon, Liz Mullan, Avis Osher, Andi Rosin, Joan Vertes, and Sue Wahl (all occupational therapists); Jean Loefflehardt, speech pathologist; and Dr. Cheryl Ackerman, psychologist, for their advice and encouragement.

Finally, we would like to thank Dr. Jean Ayres and the other occupational therapists who have contributed to the evolution of the theory of sensory integration.

A percentage from the sales of this book will be donated to support the valuable work of the Geneva Centre for Autism in Toronto.

About the Authors

Ellen Yack, B.Sc., M.Ed., O.T.

Ellen Yack has practised as an occupational therapist since 1979. She is the Director of Community Paediatric Therapy Centre, a private agency providing occupational therapy services to children, adolescents, and their families. Her areas of expertise include sensory integration, autism, and learning disabilities.

Ellen has been a lecturer at the University of Toronto, has conducted a variety of workshops and presentations, and has written numerous publications. She was the Registrar of the Ontario College of Occupational Therapists from 1987 to 1991.

Ellen provides a variety of consultation services to individuals and organizations through her private practice. She is currently the occupational therapy consultant at the Geneva Centre for Autism in Toronto, Canada. Ellen lives in Toronto with her husband, Irv Marks, and children Lia, Michael, and Robbie.

Paula Aquilla, B.Sc., O.T.

Paula Aquilla lives in Toronto with her husband Mark, daughters Katie and Ella, and a large, happy dog, Quinton. Paula is an occupational therapist who has worked with adults and children in clinical, educational, home, and community based settings. She founded the **Yes I Can! Integrated Nursery School**, the **Yes I Can! Summer Camp**, and the **I Love My Baby Program** in Toronto, where she was director for six years.

Paula was also the founding executive director of **Giant Steps** in Toronto. She is an active treating therapist who currently runs a private practice serving families with children who have special needs.

Paula gives many workshops on the use of sensory integration in the practice of occupational therapy throughout Canada and in the United States. Her practice is an approved placement for students from the University of Toronto's occupational therapy department where she is also a regular guest lecturer. Paula is a consultant to the MacMaster University occupational therapy students. She brings warmth and enthusiasm to her work with children.

Shirley Sutton, B.Sc., O.T.

For more than 20 years, Shirley Sutton has worked as an occupational therapist for children with special needs in a variety of settings, including hospitals, schools, and childcare centres. She owns and manages **Occupational Therapy for Children**, a private practice specializing in consultation, workshops, and publications.

Shirley also works part-time for Early Intervention (Community Therapy Services) in Simcoe County, north of Toronto. Shirley has previously published articles, book reviews, and several books geared to enhancing children's motor skills. Shirley lives in Collingwood with her husband Eric and children Rachel, Jon, and Martha.

Part One

Welcome!

This book provides a practical resource for parents, educators, occupational therapists, and other professionals. Our focus is on children who have a diagnosis of autism or other pervasive developmental disorders (PDD) and who experience abnormal sensory processing and impaired motor planning. We want to empower children, parents, and service providers. We'll give you some new insights into behaviour…and some strategies for increased success!

We, the authors, are occupational therapists with expertise in sensory integration and extensive experience using this approach when working with children who have various forms of pervasive developmental disorders. The idea for this book evolved as we searched for resources to provide simple activity suggestions and accommodation strategies for children in our practices. The resources were limited, so we developed our own! Our collective years of experience working with children in varied settings provided us with the opportunity to develop and evaluate the effectiveness of a wide range of ideas.

Classification of Pervasive Developmental Disorders

First we will establish the terminology that we use in this book. Autism or autistic disorder and other pervasive developmental disorders (PDD) are currently recognized as behaviourally defined developmental disabilities that are associated with neurological impairment. These disorders are diagnosed according to specific behavioural characteristics as described in the *Diagnostic and Statistical Manual of Mental Disorders, 4th Edition* (APA, 1994). According to the manual, pervasive developmental disorders are classified as a type of clinical disorder that has five subcategories. These subcategories include:

> Autistic Disorder
> Rett's Disorder
> Childhood Disintegrative Disorder
> Asperger's Disorder
> Pervasive Developmental Disorder—Not Otherwise Specified

Each of the above subcategories has specific behavioural characteristics and ages of onset. However, they each share common characteristics, including poor social skills, impaired communication, and some form of stereotypic behaviours.

This classification system and terminology has become somewhat confusing as the terms PDD and autism are often used interchangeably (Richards, 1997). For our purposes, we will use the term PDD as it is defined by the *DSM 4th Edition*. Although we recognize the importance of differentiating between the subcategories of PDD, the information presented here can apply to all forms of the disorder. We do want to state that when we review the literature, many books and articles only use the term "autism."

The History of Pervasive Developmental Disorders and Sensory Integration

In the 1940s, when Leo Kanner first coined the term "autism," he talked about a "biological impairment like physical or intellectual handicaps" (Kanner, 1943). He also discussed perceptual difficulties present in the children he was describing and commented on overreaction to loud noises and moving objects. Unfortunately, in the 50s and 60s, this recognition of autism as a biological disorder seemed to lose its importance. During this time, autism was viewed as an emotionally based disorder resulting from parenting by a cold "refrigerator mother."

In the 1970s, we thankfully saw the move back to viewing autism as a neurological impairment. Books and articles began to examine the nature of specific problem areas. Various literature focused on the social, communication, behaviour, and cognitive problems associated with the disorder. There also was a growing body of work that looked at the perceptual and sensory processing problems of people with PDD. Eric Schopler (1965) noted that many children with autism whom he observed had abnormal responses to visual, vestibular (movement), and auditory stimuli. Ornitz (1971) looked at childhood autism as a disorder of sensorimotor integration, and later on identified problems with the modulation of sensory input and motor output (Ornitz, 1973).

Carl Delacoto (1974), in his book, *The Ultimate Stranger*, put forth the hypothesis that autism resulted from a brain injury that caused perceptual dysfunction. He proposed that many of the behaviours exhibited by people with autism were attempts to normalize their nervous systems. He believed that if you could improve how the sensory systems worked, you could reduce abnormal behaviour and increase ability to attend to and complete tasks.

In the 1970s, A. Jean Ayres, an occupational therapist, published two books: *Sensory Integration and Learning Disorders* and *Sensory Integration and the Child* (1972, 1979). Ayres (1979) defines sensory integration as the "organization of sensation for use" and discusses the effects on behaviour and development when this process is impaired. In *Sensory Integration and the Child*, she offers a reader-friendly review of the theory, and she also addresses issues relevant to children with autism. The information Ayres presented supported the hypotheses that were proposed by Delacoto and Ornitz. Ayres described the behavioural problems associated with inadequate sensory integration. Many of these behaviours were consistent with Delacoto's and Ornitz's observations.

Knickerbocker (1980), another occupational therapist, also hypothesized that many behaviours exhibited by individuals with autism may be related to hyper- or hyporeactions to sensory input. She suggested that planned sensory input provided through specific activities could help normalize reactions to sensory input and improve behaviour.

Ornitz (1985, 1993) began to refine his hypotheses, and in his articles he suggested that individuals with autism have difficulty registering, modulating, and integrating sensory stimuli. He suggested that these sensory processing differences might contribute to self-stimulatory behaviours and irregularities in arousal levels.

There are now autopsy studies that may lend support to these hypotheses. Developmental abnormalities have been found in the cerebellum and limbic regions of the brains of autistic individuals (Bauman and Kemper, 1994). These regions have significant roles within the sensory integrative process, including the modulation of sensory input.

There are many books and articles that discuss the unusual responses to sensory stimuli that some children with PDD exhibit (Ayres and Tickle, 1980; Baranek and Bergson, 1994; Cesaroni and Garber, 1991; Richard, 1997; Greenspan and Wieder, 1998). Recently, adults with autism have written accounts of their experiences and have reported negative reactions and unusual sensitivities to certain stimuli (Grandin, 1986; Williams, 1992; Grandin and Scariano, 1992; McKean, 1994; Williams, 1994; Grandin, 1995; Williams 1996). Many of these firsthand accounts have validated various aspects of sensory integration theory.

In 1985 and 1986, Temple Grandin, a woman with autistic disorder, published two books that include descriptions of her sensitivity to light touch and sounds. She discusses how certain sensations, that would be harmless to others, would impact on her behaviour and emotions. For example, certain clothing textures would make her extremely anxious, distracted, and fidgety. Certain sounds would cause her to scream and cover her ears.

Grandin discusses how she craved deep-pressure touch and movement as a child and adolescent. She also tells how deep-pressure touch helps to calm and organize her nervous system and reduces her hypersensitivity to touch. As a teenager, Grandin visited a farm and spotted a "cattle chute." This piece of equipment is used to contain cattle by exerting pressure against the sides of the body. She asked to go in the chute, believing that it would provide her with the pressure she always craved. She describes how she relaxed when in the chute and how better organized her thoughts became. Grandin subsequently built her own "squeeze or hug machine."

Grandin's experiences are consistent with Ayres' and Ornitz's hypotheses about the relationship between sensory processing and behaviour. Her reported benefits of the "squeeze or hug machine" confirm the positive response to deep-pressure touch, a calming and organizing strategy frequently proposed by occupational therapists. This strategy is also suggested by Donna Williams, another woman with autistic disorder, who describes the difficulties she has with sensory processing in her two books, *Nobody Nowhere* and *Somebody Somewhere* (1992 and 1994). In her book, *Autism: An Inside-Out Approach* (1996), Williams offers many strategies to assist individuals with PDD and suggests the use of deep touch pressure as a calming technique.

Beginning in the 1970s, more and more articles in the occupational therapy literature began to address how impaired sensory integration may contribute to many of the behaviours we see in individuals with PDD (Ayres and Heskett, 1972; Ayres and Tickle, 1980; Ayres and Mailloux, 1983; Becker, 1980; Chu 1991; Clarke, 1983; Dunn and Fisher, 1983; Inamura et al., 1990; Williamson and Anzalone 1996).

There are also specific books and articles that provide intervention strategies and methods to identify sensory integration problems that can be adapted for use with individuals with PDD (Kientz and Dunn, 1996; King 1991; Oetter, Richter, and Frick, 1995; Reisman, 1993; Reisman and Gross, 1992; Reisman and Hanschu, 1992; Royeen, 1986; Slavik et al., 1984; Wilbarger, 1984; Wilbarger and Wilbarger 1991; Wilbarger, 1995; Zisserman, 1992).

What Is in this Book?

Part One explains the role of the occupational therapist with children with PDD and provides a detailed examination of the theory of sensory integration. To better understand the reasons for our recommendations, we encourage you to read Part One. Our goal was to make the theory easy to comprehend. When people are armed with knowledge, it is easier for them to adapt recommendations for the needs of individual children.

Part Two offers methods of identifying sensory integration problems in children and provides a range of strategies and activity suggestions. It presents general recommendations, specific strategies for dealing with challenging behaviours, and accommodations for completion of certain tasks. The Table of Contents and Index will help you help you navigate through Part Two.

We strongly recommend that you consult an occupational therapist before implementing any recommendations contained in this book.

Chapter 1

What Is Occupational Therapy?

This chapter illustrates the importance of having an occupational therapist on any team working with children with PDD.

Occupational therapy is a health profession concerned with how people function in their respective roles and how they perform activities. The profession focuses on the promotion, restoration, and maintenance of productivity in people with a wide range of abilities and disabilities.

The term "occupational therapist" can often be confusing. It carries the misconception that the profession's focus is on vocational counseling and job training. The word occupation as defined in *Webster's Dictionary* is "an activity in which one engages." Occupational therapists promote skill development and independence in all daily activities. For an adult, this may mean looking at the areas of self-care, homemaking, leisure, and work. The "occupations" of childhood may include playing in the park with friends, licking a popsicle, washing hands, going to the bathroom, cutting with scissors, printing at school, running, jumping, sitting at circle time, and taking swimming lessons.

Occupational therapists are university graduates who are educated in the behavioural and neurosciences. They are trained to help people develop skills and promote independence through the use of meaningful activities. The occupational therapist (OT) may provide direct services to clients through assessment and treatment. They also provide indirect services to individual clients and organizations through consultation, mediator training, education, program development, case management, and advocacy. The OT may provide these services in individual homes, childcare centres, schools, hospitals, community and private agencies and clinics, or industrial or residential facilities.

Occupational therapists are able to analyze all internal and external factors that are necessary for individuals to perform activities. Consider the first-grade student who is learning to print. To learn this task, the student must have good hand skills, good sitting posture and balance, adequate joint stability and muscle strength, good body awareness and motor planning, mature visual perceptual and visual motor skills, good attending abilities, and adequate sensory integration.

If sensory integration is impaired, a student could have difficulty printing because she may be uncomfortable with the touch of the paper against her arm or may have difficulty attending to the task because she is highly distracted by other activities in the classroom. If the student has poor motor planning abilities, she may not be able to direct the movements of the pencil to appropriately form the required letter shapes. If the student has immature sitting balance, the height of the desk and chair will have to be analyzed and possibly altered to provide maximum stability.

Occupational Therapists Are Concerned with Development of Abilities and Skills

Abilities

- Balance and postural reactions
- Muscle tone and strength
- Body awareness
- Fine motor abilities (pinches and grasps, manipulative skills, pencil and scissors use, handwriting)
- Gross motor abilities (running, jumping, climbing)
- Motor planning (ability to plan, initiate, and execute a motor act)
- Visual perception (shape recognition, visual memory)
- Visual motor integration (copying shapes, copying block designs)
- Sensory integration (response to sensory stimuli, discrimination of sensory input)
- Behaviour (arousal level, attention, problem-solving skills)

Skills

- Self-care skills (eating, dressing, toileting, bathing)
- Community living skills (use of public transportation, money knowledge, shopping)
- Pre-academic skills
- Play skills (use of toys, types of play)
- Social skills
- Pre-vocational and vocational skills
- Environmental factors
- Physical environment
- Family situation
- Community supports

Occupational Therapists Consult in the Following Areas

- Early intervention programs
- Home, school, and vocational settings
- Environmental and equipment adaptations
- Physical aids and assistive devices
- Behavioural strategies

Occupational Therapy and Children with PDD

Between the 1940s and early 1970s, the occupational therapy literature had few references to the profession's involvement with individuals with PDD. References include descriptions that focus on developing self-care and play skills and describe therapy practices that included the use of crafts, music therapy, and behaviour modification (Bloomer and Rose, 1989).

When Dr. A. Jean Ayres released her two books on the theory of sensory integration in 1972 and 1979, it had a significant impact on the practice of occupational therapy (Fisher et al., 1991). It provided a new framework for understanding factors that could interfere with an individual's ability to engage in activities. The theory of sensory integration also inspired the development of new assessment procedures and treatment strategies.

Occupational therapists began to look at how their clients responded to different types of sensations and to observe whether they could effectively organize and use sensory information. Sensory integration theory became a useful framework for occupational therapists working with clients who had PDD because so many of these clients had unusual responses to sensory stimulation.

The role of occupational therapy with individuals with PDD gained increased recognition in the 1990s primarily because of the following:

- The evolving theory and practice of sensory integration
- Investigations into the neurobiology of autism
- Firsthand accounts written by adults with autism who have described their difficulties with sensory processing

There are now many occupational therapy articles and books exploring the theory of sensory integration and its implications for individuals with PDD. Occupational therapists have become frequent speakers at PDD workshops, conferences, and association meetings. The Internet has many sites where occupational therapy-related information is shared by parents and professionals.

Our Role as Occupational Therapists

As occupational therapists, our work with children with PDD is guided by the theory of sensory integration, but it also utilizes other theories and techniques. We take a holistic view of the child and have an extensive array of strategies to rely on to meet a child's individual needs. For example, occupational therapists are trained in "task analysis" for the teaching of new skills. This technique is very important when we teach dressing, feeding, and toileting skills. To maximize learning and performance, we combine our knowledge of sensory integration theory with task analysis. When teaching new skills, we make accommodations for sensory problems or impaired motor planning.

When assessing a child with PDD, we determine what is interfering with his or her ability to engage in activities of childhood. Perhaps poor body awareness is causing immature coordination and preventing a child from learning independent feeding and dressing skills. Another child may have difficulty feeding because he or she is hypersensitive to touch and does not like how the spoon feels or does not like the texture of the food in his or her mouth.

Formal or standardized tests to assess children with PDD are not generally used because these children often do not have the attention, comprehension, or motivation to follow standardized instructions. Instead, we rely on our observations of children performing the desired activities in more informal situations or in their natural settings. We also rely strongly on parental observations and a detailed history of the child's behaviour. This information is obtained through the use of questionnaires and interviews with parents and professionals involved with the child and family.

Once we complete the assessment, we review the findings with the parents and together determine the priorities for their child. It may not be appropriate to provide occupational therapy intervention if there is only a mild delay in motor development, and sensory processing appears fairly intact. However, if impaired motor skills and/or poor sensory processing is significantly interfering with skill development and behaviour, an occupational therapist is an important member of the intervention team.

When occupational therapy intervention is required, we often recommend a combination of regular treatment sessions and home and school programming suggestions. When appropriate, we see children for ongoing treatment. Therapy sessions can facilitate more appropriate responses to sensory input and can improve body awareness and motor skills.

When consulting, we help other professionals and parents analyze specific behaviours demonstrated by children. We determine if the behaviour is related to sensory needs or motor impairment. We provide activity and programming suggestions tailored to the needs of the individual child. Some children need a "sensory diet" (see chapter 5). This is a specific schedule of sensory activities designed to help the child remain calm, relaxed, and attentive. We will also recommend techniques for feeding, toileting, and dressing to achieve and maintain independence in these and other daily living skills.

We often work with families who may be involved in specialized intervention programs. Many of the children in our practices participate in **Applied Behavioural Analysis Programs** (ABA), and we often provide recommendations to augment the program. For example, depending on a child's sensory needs, we may suggest that during breaks from ABA sessions, the child engage in rough and tumble play and jumping activities. To increase attention to tasks, we may suggest the use of a weighted vest or seating adaptations for a child participating in tabletop activities. For children involved in a floor-time program (Greenspan and Weider, 1998), or the **Miller Method** (Miller and Miller, 1989), we may suggest activities that facilitate engagement and attention.

Case Study

Rachel is a nine-year-old girl who has a diagnosis of autistic disorder. Rachel lives at home with her parents and two siblings. She is non-verbal, but she communicates using eye gaze and gestures and is beginning to use the Picture Exchange Communication System (Bondy and Frost, 1997). She has a very high activity level, has great difficulty attending to structured tasks, and initiates a limited range of purposeful activities. She engages in various stereotypic or self-stimulatory behaviours, including rocking, jumping, and hand flapping. Rachel is highly sensitive to auditory stimuli and startles to unexpected noises. She is a client of a centre that provides services to individuals with pervasive developmental disorders and their families. An occupational therapy consultation for Rachel was requested due to concerns regarding her increasing self-abusive behaviour, poor sleeping patterns, and fine motor delays.

Evaluation: The occupational therapy evaluation involved informal clinical observations, parent and teacher interviews, and the use of questionnaires. Rachel was beginning to cut into her fingers with her nails, and this behaviour was occurring increasingly at school when she was under stress. An analysis of Rachel's self-abusive behaviour was conducted using the **Durand Motivation Assessment Scale** (Durand, 1986), and the therapists thought that Rachel's motivation was the need for sensory stimulation. The **Analysis of Sensory Behaviour Inventory** (Morton and Wolford, 1994) revealed that Rachel had a strong preference for activities that offered her proprioceptive input (deep pressure to her muscles and joint compression). She jumped on couches and beds, squeezed into small spaces, wore tight clothing and hats, and squeezed against her parents for comfort.

Rachel demonstrated immature pinches and grasps that interfered with pencil and paper activities and self-care skills. Rachel had difficulty attending to tasks at home and school as she was easily distracted by sounds. Her activity level and self-abusive behaviour increased in noisy environments. Rachel's family needed to be very quiet when she slept as she would easily wake with any unexpected noises.

Intervention: Therapists used sensory integration theory as an aid in interpreting Rachel's self-stimulatory and self-abusive behaviour. Rachel might have sought out proprioceptive stimulation to help calm and organize her nervous system. It was also suspected that there was a relationship between the pressure applied to her fingers and Rachel's ability to cope with stressful situations. Alternative ways to provide pressure that were more socially acceptable and that avoided injury were therefore explored.

The therapists recommended that Rachel have regular exercise breaks at home and school, which included jumping on a mini-trampoline, playing Tug of War, and hitting punching bags. These exercise breaks were listed on her visual schedule of daily activities to help her anticipate their occurrence. Rachel was to wrap ponytail elastics around her fingers during potentially stressful events. It was important to supervise her when the elastics were on because she occasionally would wrap them too tightly around her fingers. The therapists recommended that Rachel wear a weighted vest in the classroom and at home when she needed to attend to structured tasks. Rachel also began to wear a "girdle-like" garment to bed that was designed by her mother. Proprioceptive input by these garments could help to reduce hypersensitvity to sensory stimulation.

To further develop Rachel's pinches and grasps, the therapists had Rachel start to use broken crayons when drawing and a Stetro® grip on her pencil. Rachel liked stickers, so she was encouraged to peel off small stickers and create patterns. Rachel was prompted to wrap elastic bands around pegs because she enjoyed that. This activity encouraged use of a mature pinch.

Outcome: Rachel's self-abusive behaviour significantly decreased, and her need for ponytail elastics around her fingers reduced. Her self-stimulatory behaviour also decreased as the more socially appropriate stimuli offered during exercise breaks appeared to satisfy her need for proprioceptive input. Rachel's attending behaviours improved. She began to develop early computer skills, and she was more cooperative during communication training. Rachel began to sleep through the night on a consistent basis, which she had never done before. Rachel also demonstrated improvement in pencil use and self-care skills as she was better able to grasp and manipulate objects.

Chapter 2

What Is Sensory Integration?

Picture yourself at a cottage. You are standing on the dock, about to climb into a canoe. You put your foot down into the canoe, and as you begin to step in, the canoe starts to rock. Automatically you adjust your body to keep yourself balanced and slowly sit down, placing yourself in the middle of the seat. THIS IS SENSORY INTEGRATION.

Our bodies and the environment send our brains information through our senses. We process and organize this information so that we feel comfortable and secure. We are then able to respond appropriately to particular situations and environmental demands. *THIS IS SENSORY INTEGRATION.*

Sensory integration is a neurological process that occurs in all of us. We all take in sensory information from our bodies and the world around us. Our brains are programmed to organize or "integrate" this sensory information to make it meaningful to us. This integration allows us to respond automatically, efficiently, and comfortably in response to the specific sensory input we receive. Figure 1 illustrates how the process of sensory integration contributes to development.

When stepping into that canoe, you receive information from various sensory channels. Your touch system tells you that your foot is on the bottom of the canoe. Your proprioceptive system tells you the position of your muscles and joints. Your vestibular system tells you that your centre of gravity is off and that you are on a moving surface. Your visual system determines that the canoe is lower than the dock.

If you have good sensory integration, processing and organizing this information happens automatically. You do not become overly fearful when the boat moves because you are confident that you can maintain your balance. Unconsciously you make fine adjustments and regain your centre of gravity. You can lower yourself to the seat because you judge the distance and the size of the seat. You also have a good sense of where to sit and how much to move to centre yourself on the seat.

For the child who does not have good sensory integration, climbing into a canoe can be a disaster. Some children can be afraid about the prospect of climbing into a boat because

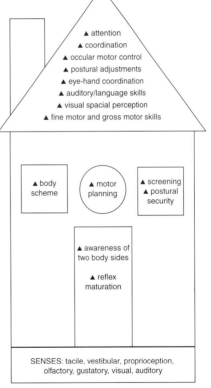

Figure 1: Sensory Integration as a Foundation for Learning
Adapted from *Sensory Integration Theory* by A. Jean Ayres, Ph.D., OTR

they are uncomfortable with, or hypersensitive to, the feeling of movement. Other children may be overconfident and may not appreciate what can happen when balancing on a moving object. They may climb into the canoe quickly, tipping the boat because they have poor body awareness and place all their weight to one side of the canoe.

through Sensory Integration

21

In recent years, the terms "sensory integration" and "sensory processing" have sometimes been used interchangeably. We use the term "sensory integration" because Dr. A. Jean Ayres used this term, and we feel it better reflects what happens in the nervous system when we receive and organize sensory information.

How Did the Theory of Sensory Integration Develop?

A. Jean Ayres first proposed the theory of sensory integration. She was an occupational practicing in a children's centre during the late fifties and early sixties, and she developed a keen interest in how the brain works. Returning to university work, Ayres earned a doctoral degree and pursued postdoctoral work. During her studies she formulated the theory of sensory integration, based on established knowledge and theories found within the neuroscience field (Fisher, Murray, and Bundy, 1991). In addition to her two books, Dr. Ayres also developed two test batteries to assist in identifying problems with sensory integration (Ayres, 1979; Ayres, 1985).

Her theory describes normal sensory integrative abilities, defines sensory integrative dysfunction, and guides intervention programs that use sensory integrative techniques (Fisher et al., 1991). This theory continues to evolve and provides a framework for intervention with children and adults with a variety of special needs. The theory of sensory integration is an important frame of reference for occupational therapy, but it is also becoming a valuable guide for other disciplines (Windeck and Laurel, 1989; Mora and Kashman, 1997).

How Does Sensory Integration Occur?

Williamson and Anzalone (1996) identify five interrelated components that help to explain how sensory integration occurs. These components are

1. Sensory registration
2. Orientation
3. Interpretation
4. Organization of a response
5. Execution of a response

1. Sensory Registration

Sensory registration occurs when we first become aware of a sensory event. "Something is touching me," or "I hear something." We may not be aware of certain types of sensory input until it reaches a certain threshold or intensity. Your "sensory threshold" varies throughout the day, depending on your previous sensory and emotional experiences, how alert or stressed you are, and what you expect.

You may not be aware of a mosquito buzzing by the window, but when it is flying around your head, you are certainly aware that you hear something. You've experienced that sound previously, and you expect the mosquito to land, creating a bite that will itch for days.

When you are highly aroused or anxious, your sensory threshold is lower, and you may register sensory input that may go ignored any other time. If you are awakened in the night by a loud "bang," you may become highly aroused and hyper-vigilant. You may notice or "register" the sounds of creaking stairs and humming fixtures that you never pay attention to during the day.

Implications for PDD

Many children and adults with PDD over-register or are hyper-responsive to sensory stimulation. Some report hearing whispers from another room or the sounds of trains that are miles away. Others report that certain clothing textures feel like sandpaper.

Kientz and Dunn (1997) compared performances of children with and without autism using **The Sensory Profile** questionnaire. The researchers found that 85% of the items on the questionnaire differentiated between those subjects with autism and those without autism. Hypersensitivity to touch and auditory stimulation were the most commonly sited items. Hypersensitivity to touch and sound is also commonly cited by adults with autism (Grandin, 1986 and 1995; McKean, 1994; Williams, 1992).

Children and adults with PDD may also under-register sensory information. They may not notice someone calling them. They may not feel pain like other people and may only respond when sensory stimulation is highly exaggerated.

Greenspan and Weider (1998) reviewed the sensory processing patterns of 200 children with diagnoses of autism spectrum disorder. They found that 94% of the children exhibited unusual sensory processing patterns (39% were under-reactive, 19% were over-reactive, and 36% exhibited a mix of over- and under-reactivity).

It is important to note that responses to sensory input may be highly inconsistent and vary on a daily basis. Also, some children who appear unresponsive to sensory input may in fact be highly sensitive to sensory stimulation. They may appear unresponsive because their nervous systems have "shutdown" to protect them from incoming sensory stimulation.

Examples of Hyper-reactivity:

- Distress with certain sounds
- Sensitivity to light
- Discomfort with certain textures
- Aversion to certain smells and tastes
- Irrational fear of heights and movement
- Frequent startle reactions

Examples of Hypo-Reactivity:

- Disregard of sudden or loud sounds
- Unaware of painful bumps, bruises, cuts, etc.

- Absence of startle reactions
- Lack of attention to environment, persons, or things
- Lack of dizziness with excessive spinning
- Delayed responses

Please refer to chapter 4 for a more complete list of observations.

2. Orientation

Sensory orientation allows you to pay attention to new sensory information being received. "Something is touching my arm" or "I hear something buzzing around my head." We are able to determine what sensory information needs our attention and what information can be ignored. This happens through sensory modulation and the functions of inhibition and facilitation.

Our brains are programmed to modulate or balance incoming sensory information to function efficiently. We cannot possibly attend to all sensory stimuli in our environments. If all sensory input had equal importance, we could not select the relevant stimuli for the specific situation.

When talking on the phone, your brain decides that the voice in the receiver is important and needs your attention. It also decides that the television sounds, the feel of your clothing and jewelry, and the placement of your hands are not as important.

Sensory modulation is necessary to regulate the brain's activity level and, therefore, our activity levels. Ayres (1979) compares the process of modulation to volume control. If the sensory information received is "too loud," "too intense," or "too insignificant," our brain can inhibit or "turn down" the flow of information. This neurological process of inhibition prevents us from attending to meaningless sensations. The process of inhibition lets us concentrate on the telephone conversation and ignore the voices coming from the television.

When we need to turn the "volume" up, we rely on facilitation. Sometimes we need help to respond to meaningful sensations, and this is when the neurological process of facilitation is activated. When sitting in a lecture and our arousal levels are low, we may not properly attend to the voice of the professor. The process of facilitation helps us to pay attention to a voice and orient to the speaker. Sensory modulation occurs unconsciously and results when there is a balance between inhibition and facilitation.

Implications for PDD

Many children with PDD have poor sensory modulation. Atypical sensory registration and orientation can interfere with the processes of inhibition and facilitation. One child may not be able to follow verbal instructions or interact with others because he or she is attending to "meaningless" sensations of wind against his or her face or dust particles in the air. Another child may be overwhelmed and uncomfortable with certain sensations, displaying fear and anxiety.

3. Interpretation

Our brains can interpret sensory information and describe its qualities. "I am being lightly touched on my arm by a piece of silk fabric." "I hear a loud, female voice telling me that it's time for dinner." The ability to interpret sensory information allows us to determine what to respond to and whether it is threatening. We compare new sensory experiences with old ones. Our language, memory, and emotional centres are involved with the interpretation process.

> *I smell something. It smells like bread baking. I like that smell. It makes me feel happy. The smell reminds me of my childhood. It is okay for me to find out where the smell is coming from.*

Your nervous system is also programmed to respond to sensory input to protect you from harm. Picture yourself at home alone, reading a book. Your husband isn't due back from his business trip until tomorrow. Suddenly, someone taps you lightly on the shoulder. Your heart immediately beats faster, your breath quickens, you are suddenly sweating, and you jump out of the chair. Your body is ready to run or strike the person who touched you. When you realize it is your husband, your body relaxes, and your breathing and heart rate return to normal.

This is the nervous system's "fright, flight, or fight" reaction that helps to protect the body from potential harm. This reaction immediately increases heart rate and respiration, diverting blood away from the digestive system to the muscles. Sometimes this reaction is appropriate. If the person tapping your shoulder was a burglar instead of your husband, you would want your body to instantly respond. If your heart rate and respiration increase and more blood flows to your muscles, you are better prepared to flee from the burglar.

Implications for PDD

Atypical language, memory, and emotional development in individuals with PDD may interfere with the ability to interpret sensory information. Sensory experiences may not be adequately labeled or remembered. Familiar, pleasurable sensory experiences may not be connected with positive emotions. Individuals with PDD may also have problems with the stages of sensory registration and orientation, subsequently hampering the interpretation process. It is difficult to interpret sensory information if our input is distorted, inconsistent, too strong, or too weak.

Sensations may constantly be interpreted as new or unfamiliar. The world can seem like a confusing place when there is no sense of familiarity. One reason that children and adults with PDD may have difficulty with transitions, and can become obsessed with order and set routines, is because they strive for predictability in a world that bombards them with different sensations that are difficult to understand. As previously mentioned, individuals with PDD more frequently report hypersensitivity to sensory input.

The term "sensory defensiveness" describes the tendency to react negatively, or with alarm, to sensations that are generally considered inoffensive (Wilbarger and Wilbarger, 1991). Children may be defensive to all types of sensory input or one specific sensation. Defensive responses may be highly variable and inconsistent. Wilbarger and Wilbarger (1991) suggest that 15% of the general population likely have mild, moderate, or severe forms of sensory defensiveness. The percentage of individuals with PDD who are sensory defensive is not known, but the numbers are likely significant, and its effect on behaviour is easily observable.

Examples of Sensory Defensive Behaviours

- Touch or Tactile Defensiveness—avoids touch from others; dislikes messy play; irritated by certain clothing textures and labels
- Gravitational Insecurity—fear and dislike of movement and changes in body position; discomfort with changes in head positions; fear of having feet off the ground
- Auditory Defensiveness—over-sensitivity to loud, unexpected, or specific sounds; fearful of appliances such as vacuum cleaners or hair dryers
- Visual Defensiveness—over-sensitivity to strong or different types of light; avoids or squints in sunlight; avoids eye contact; dislikes glare from televisions and computers
- Oral Defensiveness—a combination of over-sensitivity to touch, smell, and taste; dislikes certain food textures and types; difficulty with tooth brushing and face washing
- Other—may be oversensitive to smells and tastes; some children may gag with certain smells; can identify specific brands of food by taste

Children who are sensory-defensive operate under high levels of anxiety as they are bombarded by sensations that they do not like, and this may encourage "fright, flight, or fight" reactions. As they are often in a hyper-aroused state, they become hyper-vigilant and have lower sensory thresholds, which make them even more responsive to sensory input.

These children who are sensory defensive may avoid sensations to prevent negative reactions, but they may also seek out certain sensations as a coping strategy. Certain types of sensory input, such as deep-touch pressure, can help decrease hyper-reactive responses to sensory input. Bumping into objects, bouncing, and squeezing between pillows and furniture may be a calming or organizing strategy that the child has found successful. Some children may engage in certain types of sensory-seeking behaviours to screen out uncomfortable sensations. For example, some children create an excessive amount of noise through humming or babbling to screen out irritating or unexpected noises.

4. Organization of a Response

Our brains determine if a response to a sensory message is necessary, and we choose the response. This response can be physical, emotional, or cognitive. Remember our example regarding the mosquito landing on your body? You can choose to respond to that sensory event in different ways:

Physical Response—*"I will hit the mosquito."*

Emotional Response—*"I am anxious. I do not want the mosquito to bite me."*

Cognitive Response— *"I choose to ignore the mosquito."*

Implications for PDD

Difficulties with registration, orientation, and/or interpretation affect the ability to organize a response to sensory input. Appropriate responses to sensory input cannot be organized if the nature and meaning of the input is unclear. For some, the response may be exaggerated if the input is interpreted as being harmful. The "fright, flight, or fight" response may be activated. For others, there may be no input response because the input did not register.

Atypical cognitive and emotional development in individuals with PDD further interferes with the ability to organize a response. Their emotional reactions may be exaggerated or minimized, and they may experience problems maintaining attention, formulating and comparing choices, and initiating plans of action.

5. Execution of a Response

The execution of the motor, cognitive, or emotional response to the sensory message is the final stage of the sensory integration process. However, if there is a motor response (e.g., hitting the mosquito), that action generates a new sensory experience as the brain receives information about body movement and touch—and the process begins again.

The ability to execute an appropriate response is dependent on the previous components and adequate motor planning abilities. Motor planning is the ability to perform purposeful activities, which we will further discuss in this chapter.

Implications for PDD

Impaired motor planning ability is increasingly recognized as a feature of PDD. Greenspan and Wieder (1998), in their review of 200 cases of children diagnosed with autism spectrum disorder, reported that 100% of the children experienced some kind of motor planning problem. Impaired motor planning significantly interferes with the ability to plan and execute motor responses.

David Hill and Martha Leary (1993) offer valuable insight into many behaviours observed in individuals with PDD. They suggest a strong association between certain behaviours and specific types of motor or movement disturbances. They identify similar movement disturbances in other neurological conditions, including Parkinsonism, Tourette syndrome, and catatonia. They suggest that the movement disturbance relates to impaired motor planning and is reflected in difficulties with starting, executing, stopping, combining, and switching motor acts. Therefore, the child who appears non-compliant when given motor-related instructions, or the child who engages in perserverative or self-stimulatory behaviour, may have difficulty starting, switching, or stopping motor acts.

Impaired sensory integration may cause or contribute to these motor-planning difficulties because adequate processing of sensory information from the body and the environment is necessary to efficiently execute, regulate, and change motor activity.

What Are the Results of Sensory Integration?

Sensory integration contributes to the development of self-regulation, comfort, motor planning, motor skills, attention, and readiness to learn. We will take a closer look at two areas that may not be familiar—self-regulation and motor planning.

Self-Regulation

Self-regulation is the nervous system's ability to attain, maintain, and change levels of arousal or alertness (Williams and Shellenberger, 1994). These levels change, depending on the needs of specific situations and activities.

Arousal is our level of alertness. The ability to maintain appropriate states of arousal develops from our ability to balance (regulate or modulate) sensory input from our environment. A normal state of arousal is essential for the development of the following abilities:

- Attention to tasks
- Impulse control
- Frustration tolerance
- Balance of emotional reactions

Our state of arousal varies throughout the day. We all use various strategies to regulate our levels of arousal. For most of us, our state of arousal is fairly low when we wake up and start our morning routines. For some people, their state of arousal increases after a quick shower; some may need the caffeine boost of a first cup of coffee; and some people feel more awake after an early morning jog.

> *You are on your way to work. Your level of alertness may be reduced if you are lulled by the slow rocking of the subway train and may increase again as you step outside and are bombarded by the traffic's screeching brakes and blaring horns. After working at your desk for a couple of hours, you may experience trouble concentrating and instinctively know that a body stretch or quick walk to the water cooler will increase your state of arousal and increase your ability to concentrate on your work.*

> *It is 2:30 p.m., and you are in a meeting. The person speaking has a low voice with little animation. He's been droning on for an hour. Your boss is present, and you are starting to fall asleep. You begin using familiar strategies to keep awake—shifting slightly in your chair, popping a mint into your mouth, or fiddling with your hair.*

Strategies to enhance self-regulation take into consideration the effect that different sensations can have on the nervous system. Remember that certain types of sensations can excite the nervous system and other types of sensations can relax the nervous system.

Children with sensory integration problems often have difficulty achieving and maintaining normal levels of arousal. Normal levels of arousal are dependent on adequate sensory modulation. It is difficult to develop strategies to change arousal levels when an individual does not respond appropriately to sensory information. Arousal levels can be directly affected by reactivity to sensory input. Hyper-reactivity can increase arousal and hypo-reactivity can create insufficient arousal levels.

> *Joey is a five-year-old boy who has Asperger's. His kindergarten class just came inside from the playground, and now it is circle time. Joey is highly aroused from his high level of activity outside, but now he has to sit and attend to a story. The other children are initially slightly restless, but they soon settle down and listen to the story. Some children calm themselves down by sitting in a teacher's lap, sucking their thumbs, or twirling their hair.*
>
> *Joey is not able to settle down. He remains highly aroused. He is distracted by all of the toys he sees in the classroom. He hears the teacher's aide preparing snack at the back of the room. He wonders what smells so good and wants to see what he is having for snack. Joey wants to hear the story, but he frequently gets up from the circle, bumps into the children sitting beside him, continually adjusts his posture, and frequently speaks out loud.*

Joey has poor sensory modulation. He cannot balance incoming sensory information. He cannot decide what sensory information is important and needs his attention. Joey is not able to determine what strategy he can use to improve his ability to sit in circle and listen to the story. To assist Joey with self-regulation, specific strategies that offer deep-touch pressure can be incorporated into his routine. For example, Joey may benefit from playing Tug of War when coming in from outside, and he may be able to attend better during circle time if he wears a weighted vest.

Williams and Shellenberger (1994), in their book *How does Your Engine Run? A Leader's Guide to The Alert Program for Self-Regulation*, describe the excellent program that they developed to teach self-regulation strategies. The program teaches children and adults how to recognize their own varying levels of arousal or alertness and how these levels impact learning, behaviour, and attention. Williams and Shellenberger provide a range of strategies that can be easily taught to children and help increase or decrease arousal.

Implications for PDD

Many children and adults with PDD appear to have difficulty with self-regulation (Siegel, 1996). Problems with self-regulation may be contributing to many of the behaviours observed in individuals with PDD. These behaviours include disregard or exaggerated responses to sensory stimulation, inconsistent ability to attend to tasks, distractibility, poor impulse control, limited frustration tolerance, and fluctuating emotional reactions.

Many children and adults with PDD also operate under high levels of anxiety that increase arousal. With increased arousal, sensory thresholds are lower, and there is registration of an excessive amount of sensory input. It is important to try and determine if observable behaviours are related to sensory defensiveness or pre-existing anxiety. However, similar calming strategies may be useful in reducing anxiety and limiting sensory defensive responses.

Children with PDD, whether they are verbal or non-verbal, can learn various strategies to assist with self-regulation. These strategies are presented in Part Two of this book.

Motor Planning

Motor planning (praxis) is the process of deciding what your body has to do and then doing it. Praxis comes from the Greek word for action. Both motor planning and praxis refer to the same process that includes conceiving, planning, sequencing, and executing actions. Motor planning assists with the sensory integration processes of organizing and executing responses to sensory input. Motor planning relies on sensory feedback from the body and environment, as well as on language, memory, and cognitive or thinking skills. It is a very complex process that involves many parts and functions of the brain.

The steps involved in motor planning include

- Creating an idea
- Using sensory feedback to determine the starting position of the body
- Initiating the action
- Sequencing the steps required in the action
- Adjusting actions accordingly
- Stopping the action

Robbie sees his Barney® doll sitting on the shelf. He decides he wants to give Barney a ride in his wagon. He must stand on the tips of his toes and fully extend his arms to reach Barney. Then he must walk a short distance while he carries Barney and place him in the wagon. The wagon is quite heavy for a three-year-old boy, so Robbie must use all of his strength to pull the wagon around the room.

He moves quickly, but he is very careful and slows down when he nears a corner of the room so that the wagon won't scratch the walls. He soon begins to tire and becomes bored with this game. Robbie relaxes his muscles, stops pulling the wagon, and goes to look for Mickey Mouse®.

Robbie's actions appear so simple, but the processes that allow him to participate in this type of activity are very complex. He first had to come up with the idea of pulling Barney in the wagon. He knew that Barney and the wagon were toys, and he remembered experiencing pleasure when playing with Barney. He knew that he could physically remove Barney from the shelf, and he understood the functions of the wagon. This process is called "ideation" and involves language, cognitive, memory, and emotional components.

Motor planning also relies on the process of sensory integration. Sensory integration provides us with information from our bodies and from the environment that is needed to help us plan, execute, monitor, and adjust our movements.

Imitation is an early form of motor planning. The infant's ability to mirror gestures and facial expressions is an important milestone in child development. It is also important for motor development, as well as communication and bonding between babies and parents (Trott et al., 1993).

As infants and toddlers move and explore their world, they are bombarded by sensations. They learn how their bodies relate to objects, people, and the earth's pull of gravity. Through these sensations, they develop a body map or body scheme. Movement experiences create memories that can be relied on in the future when similar movement patterns need to be repeated. This allows us to generalize skills, so we can perform similar actions in different settings. We can also borrow from pre-existing motor plans to build new or expanded actions.

Toddlers climb up and down the stairs hundreds of times to learn about the position of their body in relation to the steps. They learn how high to lift or lower their legs. They learn what sounds the stairs make and how they feel when their feet hit the steps. Initially, they proceed slowly and are always looking down at their feet to be sure that their legs are moving appropriately. Soon they can negotiate stairs quickly and can climb the steps at daycare, at grandma's house, and on the playground slide.

Children begin to develop constructional abilities, which are another form of motor planning. This includes building with blocks to create towers, stringing beads, and arranging furniture to build a fort. Successful accomplishment of these tasks requires feedback from our bodies in relation to objects and the ability to perceive and identify the characteristics of different objects. The feed-forward and feedback components of motor planning help us to determine what will happen and what did happen when we move. With feed-forward, we can anticipate the necessary steps, strength, and speed required to complete a motor act. It is this process that helps us prepare to lift a heavy suitcase or grocery bag. Feedback is the information we receive while performing a motor act. This allows us to monitor and adjust our movements as needed.

When you learn a new skill like knitting, tennis, driving, or skiing, you initially have to exert a high degree of energy and concentration to perform the required movements. You fatigue easily, your frustration tolerance is limited, and you cannot casually engage in conversation because all of your attention needs to be directed to the task. If you have good motor planning, you sail through this learning phase quickly. You do not always have to consciously think about and plan all your movements. You can engage in the activity for extended periods while carrying on a serious conversation. Writing with your non-dominant hand can illustrate how much harder you have to concentrate when completing an unfamiliar task.

Good motor planning is very time and energy efficient. It enables us to do familiar tasks without having to think through each step. Many of us can drive home from work while planning the evening's activities and then arrive home not having remembered what streets were taken to avoid traffic. We are able to go on "automatic pilot" while we put our energy into other thought processes.

Dyspraxia (Impaired Motor Planning)

The term "dyspraxia" means difficulty in motor planning. Motor planning is a very complex process, and there are many areas where the process can break down.

The type of motor planning problem that sensory integration theory can address involves inefficient processing of information from the tactile, vestibular, or proprioceptive systems. Children with this type of motor planning problem have difficulty learning new motor tasks, but with repeated practice, their competence can improve. However, their competence often remains restricted to the particular task they practiced and does not generalize to similar activities (Fisher et al., 1991). An excessive amount of energy and concentration must be exerted to perform motor tasks, due to limited body scheme and inadequate memories for movement experiences.

Motor planning difficulties can be very frustrating and confusing. Often the child knows what he or she wants to do and understands the demand, but cannot access the motor plans necessary to accomplish the task.

It was Karen's first day at Kinder-Gym. The instructor started showing the children warm-up exercises. Karen had trouble imitating the instructor's movements. Then the children were asked to skip around the gym, and Karen had difficulty keeping up with the group. She tried to skip but was unable to alternately lift her legs. Next, the group did somersaults, which Karen was able to perform. This was one of her favorite activities that she repeatedly practiced at home. At the end of class, the children sat in a circle, and the instructor demonstrated some action songs. Karen couldn't do the actions for the "Eensy Weensy Spider" or "The Wheels on the Bus," and she was slower than the other children when playing "Head and Shoulders." Karen went home frustrated and unhappy.

Motor performance in children with motor planning problems is often very inconsistent. They may easily perform some complex actions (like a somersault) and have difficulty with seemingly simpler actions (like playing "Head and Shoulders"). Their motor abilities are significantly affected by practice, level of fatigue, and their ability to concentrate. Motor performance can vary from day to day or minute to minute. A child's inability to complete a requested task is often mistaken as poor cooperation.

Parents and teachers are often confused by the inconsistencies in motor performance exhibited by children with motor planning problems. Some children can create intricate Lego® buildings but cannot imitate simple block designs. Other children are able to paint very mature pictures but have great difficulty learning how to print. These are examples of problems with the constructional components of motor planning. Sometimes it is easier to construct buildings or draw when it is self-directed.

This is true for other aspects of motor planning. For many of us, it's easier to dance when we are leading and in control of the steps we make.

Motor planning problems affect the ability to sequence, time, and grade motor activities. The feed-forward and feedback processes of motor planning are significantly compromised when there is a sensory integration problem. Poor body awareness does not provide the information necessary to anticipate motor demands or adjust movements once executed.

Motor planning problems interfere with the performance of self-care skills because a child may have difficulty performing or sequencing actions needed to complete tasks like independently dressing. Speech production can be affected by poor motor planning by interfering with movements of the lips, tongue, and jaw necessary to form and sequence sounds and words. Motor planning problems can even spill over into academic work, as manifested in organizational difficulties.

Children with motor planning problems can demonstrate a range of behavioural responses. Many can become easily frustrated and avoid motor activities. Others will persevere with activities and will develop compensatory strategies to complete the tasks. For example, some children will talk themselves through a task and others will use visual cues. Some children are highly impulsive and try to complete tasks as quickly as possible. Others may appear inflexible as they try to direct their own actions and control the actions of others.

Children with motor planning problems may experience a sense of bewilderment. They do not have a physical disability that restricts their movement, yet they know something is different. They are not sure if they can complete tasks, even ones they have completed successfully the previous day.

Implications for PDD

There appears to be a significant percentage of children with PDD who have some form of a motor planning problem (Greenspan and Weider). Kanner (1943), in his first descriptions of autism, reported the presence of motor problems. Donnellan and Leary (1995), Hill and Leary (1993), and Attwood (1993) note that some of the movement problems experienced by individuals with PDD are similar to difficulties experienced by people with Parkinson's disease. These problems include delayed initiation of motor actions, problems stopping or changing movements, difficulty combining motor acts, and general difficulty with the execution of movement.

The cause of motor planning problems in children with PDD is difficult to identify. Contributing factors may include impairments in cognitive, language, and memory functions. For those children who exhibit impaired motor planning along with unusual responses to sensory stimulation, one of the contributing causes may be faulty sensory integration. The children may not be developing appropriate body awareness and memories for movement experiences so necessary for motor planning.

A problem with motor planning may also be a factor in some of the unusual behaviours exhibited by children with PDD. New actions require a lot of energy and concentration to learn, and children may become "stuck" in old motor plans. Some children may have difficulty stopping one action to start another action. This may help to explain some of the perseverative behaviours observed in children with PDD. If a child is only capable of a few motor plans, his choices for activities may be limited.

Interest and use of toys may be complicated by the inability to effectively manipulate the toys. Some children may not be capable of sequencing the actions of the toys that are sometimes necessary for imaginative play. Children may prefer unstructured gross motor activities like rough and tumble play instead of games that require specific or sequenced movements like games with balls and sticks.

> *Sam was involved in an applied behavioural analysis program where he made significant gains in colour and shape matching, but made limited progress in verbal or motor imitation. Sam loved to play with cars, but all he did was bang the cars on the floor. He did not put the cars on the racetrack or place figures inside the cars. He sometimes was able to push the buttons on his battery-operated cars, getting them to move, but he couldn't do this consistently. He sometimes had difficulty isolating his index finger to touch the start button, and sometimes he was not able to exert enough pressure on the button to activate the engine.*

Any evaluation procedures or treatment approaches for children with PDD must consider that these children may be experiencing motor planning problems. Experienced occupational therapists can help determine if motor planning impairments are related to sensory integration dysfunction. They can provide necessary treatment and develop strategies to accommodate or compensate for impaired motor planning.

What Is Sensory Integration Dysfunction?

Children who have inadequate sensory integration, or "sensory integration dysfunction," may have

- Inappropriate and inconsistent responses to sensory stimulation
- Difficulty organizing and analyzing information from the senses
- Reduced ability to connect or "integrate" information from the senses
- Limited ability to respond to sensory information in a meaningful and appropriate manner
- Difficulty using sensory information to plan and execute actions

Checklists to identify sensory integration problems are provided in chapter 4.

Let's briefly review some of the observable signs of sensory integration dysfunction

- Hyper-sensitivity, hypo-sensitivity, or mixed sensitivities to sensory stimulation
- Avoids sensory input
- Seeks sensory input

- Unsure of body position
- Poor motor planning
- Poor coordination, inconsistent motor performance, difficulty learning new motor tasks
- Easily distracted, limited attending skills
- Over-aroused, high activity level, hyper-vigilant
- Under-aroused, low activity level, self-absorbed, passive

Incidence and Cause of Sensory Integration Dysfunction

Currently, there is no concrete information on the incidence or causes of sensory integration dysfunction. Sensory integration dysfunction has been identified in children with various diagnoses, including PDD, cerebral palsy, learning disabilities, and hearing impairment and can be present in children with no specific diagnosis.

When you consider the general population, the efficiency of the process of sensory integration can be viewed on a continuum. Some of us are natural athletes, have excellent body awareness, are comfortable in our environments, easily adapt to change, and quickly learn new skills. Others may not keep up in aerobic classes, may bump into people and objects, dislike the feel of labels in clothing, do not cope well with change, and have difficulty learning new tasks.

Ayres (1979) estimated that five to ten percent of "normal" children experience sensory integration problems that require intervention. Intervention is required when sensory integration problems prevent children from adequately performing and participating in the activities of childhood. The causes of sensory integration dysfunction are not clear. Possible causes include immature or atypical development of the nervous system or faulty transmission of information within the nervous system.

What Does Sensory Integration Theory Offer Children with PDD?

1. Sensory Integration Increases Understanding

Sensory integration theory provides a useful framework for understanding many behaviours exhibited by children with different forms of PDD. Problems may contribute to high levels of anxiety, avoidance of people, lack of interest in the environment, difficulty with transitions, and many other behaviours. For example, if a child is hypersensitive to light touch and sounds, he may avoid people and toys as a way of protecting himself from receiving uncomfortable sensory stimulation.

Sensory integration theory can provide a framework for understanding some forms of stereotypic or self-stimulatory behaviour exhibited by many children with PDD. This framework hypothesizes that some self-stimulatory behaviour is the expression of a sensory need (King, 1991). For example, rocking, spinning, banging, jumping, scratching, or mouthing behaviours may be a reflection of an individual need for stimulation of the vestibular (movement), proprioceptive (deep-pressure), or touch systems.

All of us use various types of self-stimulatory behaviours to maintain attention and relax our nervous systems (e.g., twirling hair, mouthing pencils, tapping feet, rocking in rocking chairs, and bending paper clips). In children with PDD, these behaviours are usually more extreme and can interfere with function. The analysis of self-stimulatory behaviours can reveal what sensations are being sought (and under what circumstances).

Often more appropriate, alternate behaviours that do not interfere with function and offer the same sensory input can be substituted. Sensory opportunities can be provided throughout the day in structured home and school programs and, informally, through sensory stimuli provided during normal activities of daily living. Experts think that providing a "sensory diet," may decrease the need for these behaviours.

2. Sensory Integration Helps Guide Intervention

Intervention strategies based on sensory integration theory can help an individual to

- Regulate arousal levels
- Increase ability to attend and decrease distractibility
- Decrease anxiety
- Increase comfort in the environment
- Decrease stereotypic or self-stimulatory behaviours
- Develop internal motivation
- Facilitate positive interactions with peers and adults
- Promote communication
- Improve performance of a variety of skills and increase independence

An important goal of sensory integration intervention is to assist children in achieving a state of calm alertness. Once arousal levels are regulated, interventions that focus on communication, socialization, and skill development have a better chance for success. Many children with PDD have difficulty attending to tasks and learning new skills because they operate at high levels of arousal and anxiety and over-react to sensory stimuli. Other children do not respond because they are under-responsive to stimuli or overly selective of stimuli.

A regime of sensory-based activities ("sensory diet," see chapter 5) can be effective in regulating arousal levels. Following close observation and history taking, this individualized schedule of sensory activities can be incorporated into daily life and help to improve responses to sensory stimuli.

King (1991) notes that the most effective calming strategies for children with PDD are deep-touch pressure and rhythmic-vestibular (movement) stimulation. Techniques can be introduced into the home and the classroom with the use of rocking chairs, swings, weighted vests and collars, Lycra® body suits, anti-stress squeeze balls, or padded chairs.

The child may need regular treatment sessions with an occupational therapist to further assist in facilitating more normal responses to sensory stimuli and enhance the organization of sensory information. The goal of therapy is to provide and control sensory input so that the child can spontaneously and appropriately form responses that require integration of those sensations (Ayres, 1979).

Emphasis in treatment is not on specific skill development but on enhancing sensory integrative functions. Sensory-based activities, whether provided during treatment sessions or through home and school programs, are always purposeful and require the active participation of the child.

Another goal of treatment is to assist in the development of motor skills. Many children with PDD have inadequate knowledge about how they move and where they are in space. Development of fine and gross motor skills may be delayed due to impaired motor planning; limited attending skills; reduced motivation to complete tasks; fear of, and discomfort with, exploring the environment; and an over-involvement in stereotypic behaviours.

3. Sensory Integration Assists Parents and Professionals

Sensory integration theory offers

- A different perspective for understanding behaviour
- Solutions to improve behaviour
- Strategies to increase attention, motivation, communication, and interaction
- Physical and environmental accommodations
- Programming strategies

Sensory integration theory offers important insights and tools to help children with PDD perform everyday activities. Together with parents, occupational therapists can develop a variety of activity suggestions and modifications to self-care routines for a child that can improve comfort, compliance, and independence.

For example, the modification of eating utensils may help the child who overreacts to touch. Ensuring proper chair and table heights are important for the child who is uncomfortable when his or her feet are off the ground. The use of deep-pressure as a calming strategy prior to bedtime and sleeping in a sleeping bag with a body pillow prepares and encourages the child to sleep.

Sensory integration theory can assist other professionals in their work with individuals with PDD. Speech-language pathologists and behavioural psychologists can maximize the outcomes of their interventions with strategies that reduce their clients' anxiety levels and optimize their attention. For example, swinging on a platform swing can often reduce anxiety and increase eye contact and attention to tasks. The vestibular or movement stimulation provided by the swing may have an organizing effect on the nervous system and may facilitate communication.

Introduction of communication programs while swinging on a platform swing can be a useful strategy for children who are not succeeding during traditional speech-language therapy sessions. The combination of sensory integration and communication strategies is a growing theme, evident in the literature and at conferences on PDD (Cimorelli et al., 1996; Mora and Kashman, 1997).

The "floor-time" approach developed by Stanley Greenspan and Serena Wieder (1998) recognizes the importance of attention to individual sensory and motor needs in both the assessment and programming phases of intervention. This approach involves techniques to encourage playful interactions with a goal of developing new emotional and intellectual capacities (Greenspan and Wieder, 1998).

Some children involved in programs based on applied behavioural analysis (ABA) may achieve longer periods of compliance and increased attention to tasks if their sensory needs are considered when engaging in structured activities. Movement breaks, which focus on specific types of sensory stimulation, and the use of weighted vests, padded chairs, or Lycra body suits can help to reduce anxiety and increase attention, thereby maximizing a child's participation in discrete trial training sessions.

Consultation with educators can help maximize participation in the learning process at school. Sensory activities can be incorporated into classroom routines and are particularly useful during transition times. For example, when children arrive at school, or after recess or lunch, calming and pleasurable activities can be offered to achieve a level of calm alertness.

What Does Sensory Integration Theory Not Offer?

Sensory integration theory does not provide all the answers and does not offer a cure. It can help to explain some behaviours and offers strategies for intervention.

Please recognize that this framework provides only one piece of the PDD puzzle. Behaviours that initially appear sensory-related may be due to several other issues. Repetitive movements may represent a sensory-seeking behaviour designed to reduce anxiety, or they may be involuntary tics or a reflection of obsessive-compulsive tendencies.

Children with PDD have a multi-system disorder that affects all areas of development. Knowledge of cognitive, language, behaviour, and emotional development is equally important when devising programs for children with PDD.

What about Research?

We wish that we could report extensive research on sensory integration; however, very little has been done in this area. Studies have been conducted to investigate various aspects of sensory integration theory (Ayres, 1972; Ayres, 1989), but very few studies have looked at the use of a sensory integration-based treatment programs for children with autism.

Wolkowicz et al. (1977) reported improved behaviour and social skills in four children diagnosed with autism following four months of occupational therapy treatment that used a sensory-integrative approach. Ayres and Tickle (1980) studied ten children with autism and reported that the children who were hyper-reactive to sensory input responded better to treatment utilizing sensory integration techniques. Improvement occurred in behaviour, socialization, and communication. However, sample sizes for these studies were quite small, and the methodology had areas for improvement.

Some individual case studies demonstrate the effectiveness of sensory integration strategies (Ayres and Mailloux, 1983; Grandin, 1992; Larrington, 1987). Other studies report on the use of sensory integration on language development (Benaroya, Klein, and Monroe, 1977; Cimorelli et al., 1996) and on decreasing self-stimulatory behaviours (Bonadonna, 1981; Bright et al., 1981; Brocklehurst-Woods, 1990; Duker and Rasing, 1989; Iwasaki and Holm, 1989).

Kientz and Dunn (1997) have attempted to validate the use of **The Sensory Profile** checklist with individuals with PDD. They compared the performance of children with and without autism on **The Sensory Profile**. The results indicated that 85% of the items were able to differentiate the sensory processing abilities of children with autism from those children without autism.

Judith Reisman, at the University of Minnesota, is currently investigating methods to evaluate the biological responses that occur in people who overreact to certain sensory stimulation. Her results will provide useful information and will help other studies designed to measure treatment effects.

Miller and McIntosh (1998) are currently investigating the nature of sensory modulation disorders and are evaluating the effectiveness of a sensory integrative framework in the treatment of this disorder.

Although empirical research is limited, there are indications from various sources that we are on the right track. As previously noted, autopsy studies in the brains of children with autism have identified atypical development in the areas of the brain that are important in the process of sensory integration. Adults and children diagnosed with PDD are increasingly reporting their difficulties with processing sensory information and are validating the intervention strategies proposed by occupational therapists. Parents also recognize the effectiveness of sensory integration strategies in improving behaviours and developing skills.

Everyday, we see the value and effectiveness of the strategies contained in this book. We hope that future research will validate this approach. Currently, it is very difficult to conduct scientific research on children with PDD because causes are not known, the nervous system differences are not yet fully appreciated, and the diagnosis is based on behavioural characteristics.

Even within the same subcategories of PDD, presenting behaviours are highly variable, and we do not know exactly what happens in the brain to cause these behaviours. Interventions that are effective for one child may not be effective for another, even though his or her behaviours may be very similar.

To parents and professionals: please take the information presented in this book and see if it makes sense for the individual child you are living or working with. Try some strategies and observe for changes. Sometimes no changes will be observed because the approach did not meet the needs of the specific child. Sometimes the approach directly addresses the child's needs and can provide bridges for facilitating understanding and change. For some children, the changes are subtle and, for others, they can be very dramatic and can significantly improve the child's and family's quality of life.

Chapter 3

What Are the Sensory Systems?

Sensory integration theory addresses all of the sensory systems but focuses primarily on the vestibular, tactile, and proprioceptive systems. Let's look at these systems and briefly review what happens when sensory integration functions efficiently and then see what happens when a child's sensory integration is inefficient.

Children with or without a diagnosis of PDD can have problems with the tactile, vestibular, or proprioceptive systems and can exhibit similar responses and behaviours. However, children with PDD have other impairments that may contribute to their sensory problems.

The Tactile System

> *The mother feels her unborn child kick against her tummy. She quickly summons her children to come and feel her unborn baby kick. Everyone experiences a sense of wonder and amazement as the tiny kicks push against their hands. They have all experienced the miracle of life through their sense of touch. Even the unborn infant has experienced the sensation of amniotic fluid swishing around the body and the vibrations of the mother's digestive system.*

The tactile system provides us with our sense of touch. It is the first sensory system to operate in the uterus (Fisher et al., 1991), and it is important that this sense works efficiently from birth. Newborn infants have reflexes necessary for survival that can be stimulated through touch. The sense of touch enables them to turn their faces to nipples bearing milk, start bonding with their parents, and feel calmed by warm soft blankets when falling asleep. The sense of touch is important for growth and development, as well as survival. Premature infants who are regularly massaged are more alert, active, and calm and have increased weight gain and better orienting responses (Ackerman, 1991).

> *Katie was two-weeks-old and cried whenever she was hungry. Her mother picked her up and nestled her against her breast. Katie felt the nipple touch her cheek. This touch stimulated the rooting reflex that automatically turned Katie's head in search of food. As soon as Katie felt the nipple touch her lips, she latched on and began to suck. Initially, Katie needed to feel the nipple against her cheek in order to know which direction to turn her head and needed to feel the nipple in her mouth in order to begin sucking.*

The tactile system receives information about touch from receptor cells in the skin. These receptors are all over our bodies, providing information about light touch, pressure, vibration, temperature, and pain. Feedback from the tactile system contributes to the development of body awareness and motor planning abilities. Every activity of daily life, including dressing, hair and teeth brushing, eating, toileting, household chores, schoolwork, and job tasks, are dependent upon a functional tactile system. As with all sensory systems, the tactile system has both protective and discriminative abilities that complement each other throughout our lives.

The protective system is more primitive. It alerts us when we are in contact with something that may be dangerous and triggers our bodies to react against potential harm. Carol Kranowitz (1998) in her book, *The Out-of-Sync Child: Recognizing and Coping with Sensory Integration Dysfunction*, labels the protective system as the "Uh-Oh!" system. This is a very suitable label, as it illustrates the response that the protective system can generate. Sometimes the nervous system is gently alerted, and other times the "fright, flight, or fight" response is activated.

> *You're sitting around a campfire. A mosquito lands on your leg. The light touch alerts you to potential harm, and you slap your leg in an effort to avoid the mosquito's bite.*

The discriminative system enables us to feel the quality of the item we are touching. The ability to feel the soft touch of a parent, the fuzzy skin of a peach, the bumpy surface of a strawberry, and the piano keys under our fingers are all dependent upon the discriminative system. Kranowitz (1998) refers to the discriminative system as the "Ah-Hah!" system because it provides us with the details about touch.

> *Lia reached into her handbag for her keys. It was late, and she didn't want to turn on the light and disturb her family. Her fingers found one set of keys on a plastic key ring. She immediately let this go, as it was the keys to her car. Her fingers then touched the hard, metal surface of her home keys, and she immediately retrieved them from her purse, opening the door without disturbing her family.*

Initially, our protective system is dominant, but as the nervous system matures we begin to increasingly rely on the discriminative system. Newborn infants are more easily irritated by light touch, and their ability to use their sense of touch to explore the environment is limited. As the infant matures, this ability increases and becomes necessary for learning and brain development. The discriminative system becomes a vital transmitter of information, and the protective system remains ready to respond to any potential threats.

Successful function of the tactile system depends on the balance between both the protective and discriminative systems. When the sensory integrative processes of registration, orientation, interpretation, and sensory modulation are intact, we automatically know which touch is alarming, which touch is pleasurable, which touch can be ignored, and which touch needs to be explored.

Tactile Dysfunction

Children with a dysfunctional tactile system may be hyper- or hypo-sensitive to touch or may have problems with tactile discrimination.

Some children may excessively register and orient to touch input. They may have problems with sensory modulation and be unable to inhibit or screen out touch sensations. Consequently, they are always aware of the feel of their clothes against their skin, their hair against their necks, and their glasses resting against their noses. They may have difficulty shifting attention to other sensations, like the sound of a human voice, because they are so overwhelmed by messages about touch.

Some children interpret and react to harmless light touch as being potentially dangerous. Physicians and therapists often describe children as being tactile defensive with their protective systems working overtime. Many touch sensations are regarded as threatening and something to be avoided. A child may have no difficulty touching objects or people but cannot tolerate receiving touch that is not self-directed. Behaviourally, these children may appear anxious, controlling, aggressive, unwilling to participate in home and school activities, and inflexible in order to control the touch input received from the environment. The constant feeling of being vigilant or on guard and the frequent experience of the "fight, flight, or fright" response consumes a lot of energy. Subsequently, there is less energy and attention for learning and interacting.

> *Every time Sarah's mother tried to brush her teeth, Sarah became upset and screamed. Her mom had to restrain her on her lap and hold her jaw still in order to get the toothbrush into Sarah's mouth. Brushing had to be done quickly (and with a great deal of pressure), or Sarah would bite the toothbrush and try to run away. She responds similarly to nail cutting, hair brushing, and washing. Sarah refuses to learn to do these activities independently. Her mother cannot understand why these activities create so much distress.*

Other children are under-responsive to touch. They may have low arousal levels and may not register or orient to touch sensations unless they are very intense. These children do not get appropriate feedback about where they are being touched, significantly interfering with the development of body awareness and motor planning. For example, feeding and speech problems may be related to hypo-responsive touch systems. It is difficult for the tongue to move food or form sounds if there is lack of awareness of the parts of the mouth. Consider what it feels like for a few hours after your mouth is frozen at the dentist. You often slur your words, and food drips out of your mouth when eating.

Some children may experience poor tactile discrimination. They register touch but seem unable to determine the features of what they are touching. They have difficulty discriminating between textures, have problems using their sense of touch to search for objects in a drawer or a purse, and do not develop memories for touch experiences. Knowledge of how things feel contributes to our ability to manipulate objects. Poor tactile discrimination can contribute to problems with body awareness and motor planning. Think about how difficult it is to manipulate objects when you are wearing thick woolen gloves.

Max's fine motor skills were developing slowly. He had difficulty with buttons and zippers. He could not learn how to tie his shoes because the laces kept falling out of his hands. He had a limited attention span for fine motor activities because he consumed a lot of energy using his vision to confirm when objects were in his hand.

Some children who are under-responsive to touch may also have a delayed reaction to touch. For example, pain from a cut or a burn may be felt hours after it has occurred and not at the time it happened. This is a real safety concern. For most of us, if an action harms us, we immediately feel pain and discontinue the activity. If a child is unable to immediately experience discomfort or pain, the activity may be continued, producing increased injury.

Michael and his class went to a conservation area for a class trip. They decided to walk through a stream in bare feet to cool off. Immediately after entering the stream, screams could be heard from Michael's class-mates who quickly scrambled on to the grass. There were sharp stones in the stream that had cut the children's feet. Michael was enjoying the swish of the water around his feet and continued to walk in the stream. When his teacher asked him to come out of the water to check his feet, Michael was surprised to see the cuts on his feet. Later, at home, Michael would not let his mom wash his feet because they hurt.

Some children seem to seek out excessive amounts of touch sensations. Their arousal levels may be turned on low, and they crave touch in order to provide necessary input to their nervous systems. These children may touch everything, including re-peatedly stroking mom's hair, rubbing the teacher's pantyhose, and touching the fancy knick-knacks on grandma's bookshelf. Safety can also be an issue for these children. Often the desire for touch causes them to be impulsive in their pursuit of touch, and they do not take the time to ask themselves, "Is this harmful?" or "Do I need permission?"

The importance of touch in a child's life cannot be overstated. The inability to re-spond appropriately to touch sensations can seriously interfere with the ability to develop many skills. For those children who react uncomfortably to touch, the im-pact on social and emotional development is disastrous.

The Vestibular System

The baby's cries awakened his parents at three a.m., and the father went to his son's room, gently picking up the baby. Immediately, the baby's cries changed from screams to sobs. The father held his son and sat in the rocking chair, rocking slowly as the sobs subsided. The baby soon fell back to sleep. Later that day, while in a long line at the bank, the father noted that he had only five minutes to get back to work. He felt the anxiety that we all know with so much to do and so little time. The father started to rock his body back and forth while standing in line. He smiled to himself as he recognized that he was calming his nervous system in the same way he had calmed his son's the night before.

The vestibular system provides information about movement, gravity, and changing head positions. It tells us that we are moving or remaining still, as well as the direction and speed of our movement. It helps to stabilize our eyes when we are moving and tells us if objects around us are moving or remaining still. We develop our relationship to the earth through the vestibular system. Even without our eyes, we are able to determine if we are vertical or horizontal.

The vestibular system is fundamental to all our actions. Ayres (1979) suggests that the vestibular system has a critical role in the modulation of all other sensory systems. She noted that the vestibular system assists with the processes of inhibition and facilitation (see chapter 2). Remember, this is the process described as "volume control," where sensory information is turned up or down depending on specific needs and situations. This ability to balance incoming sensations assists with self-regulation and allows us to maintain appropriate levels of arousal.

We need to accurately process vestibular information to properly use our vision, prepare our posture, maintain balance, plan our actions, move, calm ourselves down, and regulate our behaviour. The vestibular system develops before we are born, and feedback from this system continues to be utilized and refined throughout our lives. The receptors for the vestibular system are located within structures of our ears (the semi-circular canals, the utricle, and the saccule). As fluid moves in the ear, it displaces strategically placed hair cells in these structures that can detect changes in gravity and different types of movement.

The vestibular system has a very strong relationship with the auditory system. Both systems respond to vibration. In primitive animals, these two systems were anatomically and functionally connected. Auditory or hearing receptors evolved out of gravity receptors, and some neural connections remain today (Ayres, 1979). Parents and occupational therapists frequently observe increased vocalization and expressive language when a child is engaged in some movement activity. Babies often babble more when they are swinging, and children with language delays often are able to produce more words when jumping, running, or rumbling. Ayres (1979) suggests that this occurs because of the links between the auditory and vestibular systems.

The visual system and the vestibular system also have a close relationship. The vestibular system influences the development of eye movements, including tracking and focusing. Together, the vestibular and visual systems help the body maintain an upright posture.

Information from the vestibular system is necessary for muscle tone, the "readiness" of a muscle to perform work. Muscle tone is necessary for posture and movement, and the ability to generate muscle tone is essential for doing activities that require more strength.

The vestibular system has both protective and discriminative functions. In the new-born, movement can stimulate reflexes designed to prevent falling. As the brain develops, there are more mature reactions designed to protect the body from harm. Toddlers who are learning to walk and are frequently tripping register the pull of gravity and sense when they are falling. Automatically, they extend their arms to protect their head and body from the fall. The adult who is standing in a canoe registers that the boat is unsteady and can automatically gain stability by moving his feet further apart and sitting down to lower his centre of gravity.

The vestibular system can discriminate between acceleration, deceleration, and rotary movements. It can detect movements that are slow, fast, or rhythmic. Some vestibular sensations, such as slow rocking, can be calming. Other vestibular sensations, like quick movements, can excite the nervous system.

Vestibular Dysfunction

Some children experience difficulty in processing information from the vestibular system. These children can be hypo- or hyper-responsive to vestibular sensations or have mixed sensitivities.

Children who overreact to vestibular sensations are fearful with any changes in gravity and position. They interpret these changes as being potentially harmful. Often these children are seen as being "gravitationally insecure." They do not like heights or when their feet are off the ground, and they do not like when their centre of gravity is displaced. These situations can trigger a sensory defensive response and activate the "fright, flight, or fight" reaction. Some children are so sensitive to changes in gravitational demands that they will get down on their hands and knees to go through a doorway, manage a change in floor surfaces, or negotiate stairs. The fear they experience is very real. They avoid climbing stairs, riding bicycles, and playing on playground equipment. Some children cannot even tolerate changes in head position, particularly when tipped back.

> *Saied quietly sat in the bathtub watching his rubber ducky bobbing in the water. Grandpa was about to wash Saied's hair, and he began to tip Saied backwards to put his head in the water. Saied screamed in terror! Grandpa's eyes widened in alarm! What had he done to hurt his grandchild? He tried again, reassuring Saied and moving slower. Saied screamed again. Grandpa decided to wash Saied's hair by putting a facecloth over his eyes and pouring water over his head while he was sitting. Saied didn't like it, but he preferred it to leaning back in the water.*

Some children feel discomfort with certain types of movement but do not feel threatened. These children can become dizzy or nauseated with movement. They may become sick or uncomfortable with the movement of cars, elevators, swings, or carnival rides.

Hyper-responsive reactions to movement and changes in gravitational demands have a negative impact on development. Activities of childhood, including tree climbing, gym skills, midway rides, boat rides, and rollerblading cause a great deal of anxiety and tend to be avoided. The desire to avoid movement has a negative effect on physical exploration of the environment. When a child does not explore the environment, gross and fine motor skills are not practiced and can become delayed. When actions are not practiced, they cannot be committed to memory, negatively affecting the development of motor planning. Children with gravitational insecurity often prefer and are more skilled doing fine motor activities because they can be practiced in a stable, movement-free position.

When children interpret something as scary or uncomfortable, they try to avoid it. They may become anxious and insecure. Controlling, inflexible behaviour is often the strategy used to prevent unpredictable movement. Children may resist participating in many activities at home and school. Interactions and social skill practice in the playground and schoolyard become limited because they avoid physical activity, creating self-imposed isolation. Vestibular sensations, such as rocking or rhythmical movement, which are so calming and organizing for the child with a functional nervous system, can be terrifying and disorganizing for a child who is hypersensitive to movement.

At the opposite end of the spectrum is the child who craves movement. This child is always on the go and does not seem able to sit still. Climbing, bumping, jumping, falling, and tumbling are common for these children. They may not appropriately register movement, or their nervous systems may require an excessive amount of movement to stay alert and organized. Children may be so motivated to move that it is very hard for them to maintain attention for any length of time. They have difficulty staying at the dinner table, sitting in circle for a story, or completing work at their desk. Their desire to move compromises their ability to attend and learn new skills.

> *Ella jumped up from morning circle and ran for the block corner. She climbed up on the slide and jumped down. The assistant got up to follow Ella and bring her back to circle. Ella happily returned but only sat for a moment, and then she was off again. Ella rarely sat through snack. She would take a nibble of food, walk around the table, and then come back for another nibble. When Ella was allowed to sit in a rocking chair for circle and snack time, her ability to remain seated improved significantly.*

Children may seek certain types of movement to screen out uncomfortable sensations from other sensory systems. Slow rocking; linear motions; and repetitive, rhythmic movements have a calming effect on the nervous system and can decrease hyperreactive responses to sensory input.

Children who are hypo-responsive to vestibular input may not recognize the demands of gravity or adequately register the qualities of movement. These children often need close supervision during play because they may not appreciate the risks that they are taking when climbing and jumping. Recognition and preparation for necessary balance reactions, motor planning, and grading of movements does not always occur. Movements may not be well planned or controlled, and children receive insufficient feedback in order to modify movements.

Shawna loved walking on the raised flagstone border of Catherine's
garden. At the corner of the garden, Shawna, who usually traveled too
quickly, would fall off the edge of the flagstones into the flowers. Catherine
would caution Shawna to slow down. Shawna continually walked along
the border and fell into the flowers. Catherine would wonder why
Shawna made the same mistake over and over again.

Shawna may not be appropriately registering and orienting to changes in gravitational demands. She may not be aware that her centre of gravity has changed, and if she does not move her body accordingly, she will fall into the flowerbed. Shawna may not adequately register, orient, or interpret feedback from her body to help master the demands of her environment. She may have difficulty forming a motor plan and cannot correct or adjust her actions.

Vestibular dysfunction can contribute to problems with self-regulation as it has a role in the modulation of all sensory systems. Inconsistent responses to sensory input, emotional instability, inappropriate arousal levels, and difficulty maintaining and shifting attention may be behavioural features of vestibular dysfunction.

The ability to master the demands of gravity is a key accomplishment in human development. Children need to achieve this milestone to develop a strong sense of security. They need to be comfortable with movement to experience the many joys of childhood that are so important for development.

The Proprioceptive System

The typist moves her fingers over the keypad while looking at the letter
to be typed. The skier shifts his body weight over his skis to perform
turns while looking at the markers ahead. The cyclist maneuvers her
bicycle through the traffic while watching for pedestrians and cars.

The proprioceptive system helps us accomplish the above feats. Proprioception is the unconscious awareness of body position. It tells us about the position of our body parts, their relation to each other, and their relation to other people and objects. It communicates how much force is necessary for muscles to exert and allows us to grade our movements. Receptors for the proprioceptive system are located in muscles, tendons (where the muscles attach to bone), ligaments, joint capsules (the protective lining of each joint), and connective tissue.

There are also "mechanoreceptors" in the skin that respond to stretch and traction. The receptors of the proprioceptive system respond to movement and gravity. Fisher et al. (1991) suggest that you really cannot separate the vestibular and proprioceptive systems because many of their functions overlap.

We depend on our proprioceptive system to help us make sense of touch and movement experiences. When you hold a square block in your hand, your skin and the position of your muscles and joints around the block provide information about shape. When we sit in the spinning teacup ride at a fair, our vestibular system, in combination with the proprioceptive system, tells us that our body is sitting still inside a spinning teacup.

An efficient proprioceptive system provides us with the unconscious awareness of our body. This awareness helps create a body scheme or a body map. We can consult this body map to determine the starting and ending position of our body during an activity. This position can be committed to memory and accessed again in the future. A usable body map and memories of movement contribute to the development of motor planning abilities. Remember, motor planning is the ability to create, organize, sequence, and execute motor actions.

Certain types of proprioceptive sensations can help the brain regulate arousal states (Wilbarger, 1991; Williams and Shellenberger, 1994). These proprioceptive sensations are provided by activities that require muscles to stretch and work hard. These activities include play wrestling, Tug of War, hitting punching bags, pulling heavy wagons, and chewing crunchy foods. Proprioceptive sensations rarely overload the nervous system, and some sensations can have both calming and alerting abilities, depending on the individual nervous system (Williams and Shellenberger, 1994).

For example, if you have been working at your desk for a long time and are beginning to fall asleep, you may decide to stand up and stretch your body to help you become more alert. Other times you may be working at your desk and are anxious because you are unsure if you are able to make a deadline. Standing up and stretching helps you relax and decreases your anxiety.

Proprioceptive input can help decrease hyper-reactive responses to other sensations. Many of us unconsciously use proprioceptive input to screen out uncomfortable sensations. When you are in a dentist's chair, and the needle to numb your mouth is piercing your gums, you grasp and squeeze the arms of the chair to block out the pain. When the professor is writing on the chalkboard and keeps breaking the chalk (making those awful sounds), you tense your shoulders, arms, and hands and grind down on your teeth to block out the noise.

Proprioceptive Dysfunction

Some children do not adequately receive or process information from their muscles, joints, tendons, ligaments, or connective tissue. This results in insufficient feedback about movement and body position. They must use vision to compensate for poor body awareness, and they have poor grading of movements. Motor planning abilities can be compromised, and fine and gross motor skills may be delayed. Proprioceptive dysfunction is usually accompanied by problems with the tactile or vestibular systems (Fisher et al., 1991; Kranowitz, 1998).

> *Liam was always crashing into things. He would crash into his classmates when lining up at the door. When he held the door open for his teacher, he would push too hard on it, and the door would crash into the wall. He had difficulty colouring because he would always press too hard and rip the paper.*

Some children cannot position their bodies correctly to get on a bicycle or step on an escalator. Once in an activity, it may be difficult to change their body position in response to demands of the activity. When playing ball, it may be difficult for some children to move right, left, or up high to catch a ball coming from different places. Some children have difficulty playing with toys because they are unsure of how to adjust their bodies to appropriately move or adjust toy parts. Children with proprioceptive problems often appear clumsy. They may fatigue easily and appear inattentive because they have to work hard and concentrate to determine the position of their bodies.

One indicator of difficulty in processing proprioceptive input is the inability to determine the amount of the force necessary to hold or move things. Frequently, objects are inadvertently broken. Written work can be messy. Writing can be too light and difficult to read or much too heavy and laborious.

> *Mira had difficulty managing any tool in her hand. Her toothbrush often fell from her hand as she tried to brush her teeth. She couldn't seem to maneuver the hairbrush and often brushed her hair with the back of the brush. She held her pencil too loosely and seemed to have difficulty putting enough pressure through her pencil tip. Her letters appeared faint and poorly formed. Mira used her vision to direct her movements and to control objects in her hands. She could not print while looking at the blackboard or a book.*

Children who are under-responsive to proprioceptive input may seek out additional proprioceptive sensations to increase their knowledge of where their bodies are in space. This additional input can increase body awareness and one's sense of security.

> *Kumiko would lean up against any person or object that might offer her support. At circle time, she always leaned on her neighbor, much to the dislike of her classmates. At her desk, Kumiko leaned against the edge with her tummy and was often seen supporting her head with her hand. She was unable to walk down the middle of a hall but would drag her hand or roll along the wall.*

There are some children who constantly seek out proprioceptive input because they are not adequately receiving and processing this input, or because they are using proprioceptive stimulation to reduce hypersensitivity to other sensations. These children often like to rock and bang their backs and heads against the couch or the chair. They may like to jump on beds and couches, squeeze between furniture, and hide under heavy blankets. Parents and teachers of children with PDD report these types of behaviours frequently.

> *Tom was hypersensitive to touch and sounds, but he liked to be squished and cuddled. He pushed against everything. He loved roughhouse play and could only sleep when the blankets were pulled tightly around him. When he was frustrated, angry, or disorganized, Tom would push his chin into the arm, back, or leg of his parents. Tom's parents often gave*

him back rubs to help him stay calm. He would find tight spaces to climb into and would often bury himself under pillows. Tom's search for pressure seemed to occupy most of his time and energy.

Tom's search for proprioceptive input may be his attempt to provide sensations that his nervous system needs to stay calm and organized. The deep-touch pressure may also help to reduce his hyper-reactive responses to touch and sounds.

The ability to respond appropriately to proprioceptive input is critical for motor development. Many children instinctively use proprioceptive input to help regulate their nervous systems. This is a useful strategy that parents, teachers, therapists, and others can easily teach children to incorporate into their daily routines.

Chapter 4

Part One investigated the role of occupational therapy with children with PDD and examined the theory of sensory integration. Part Two will offer you a method to assess possible sensory integration dysfunctions. A wide range of strategy and activity suggestions, strategies for challenging behaviours, and accommodations are provided. We hope you find what you are looking for.

Identifying Problems with Sensory Integration

How Do We Know if a Child Has a Sensory Integration Problem?

Sensory integration, the use of sensory information for function, is a process that begins prior to birth and continues right through our lifetime. Sensory integration is fundamental to self-care, play, and work. We organize and use sensory information automatically; we never really think about it. This automatic process frees us to be able to focus our attention on other tasks.

The diversity among children with PDD encourages parents and professionals to look for uniqueness in each child. We must assume the role of "detectives" in our search for clues to understand behaviours and collect observations to be analyzed across environments. Possible conclusions are formulated that provide the basis for potential intervention strategies. Observations of behaviours help us identify recurring behaviours and troublesome environments. In order to determine where sensory integration is breaking down, we need to look at every sensory system.

Sensory Histories and Profiles

Obtaining a sensory history and profile is the most vital way to evaluate sensory integration. This process identifies the sensory-related behaviours and the settings and situations in which they occur. Formal assessments are generally not useful because they do not provide information about how a child responds in natural situations. Children are often anxious during formal testing, and their responses to sensations may not represent typical reactions. This is particularly true for children with PDD, who along with being anxious, may not comprehend instructions or expectations and may not be motivated to cooperate.

Every day, parents evaluate sensory integration without recognizing it and without having the language to describe their observations.

> *"Annie has always been a poor sleeper and wakes very easily with the slightest noise. The sign on my front door says, 'Please don't ring the bell, baby sleeping.'"*

"I can't vacuum or blow my hair when David is home because he covers his ears, screams, and runs in circles."

"Adam seems fine in the grocery store until we get to the frozen food section, and he hears the buzzing of the refrigerator units."

These parents have identified that their children have unusual responses to auditory stimulation. Recording these observations forms a sensory history and profile that can come from using published questionnaires or informal checklists. An interview to discuss answers to the questionnaires or checklists should always follow.

Published Questionnaires

Reisman and Hanschu's "Sensory Integration Inventory—Revised for Individuals with Developmental Disabilities" (1992) looks at responses to vestibular, tactile, and proprioceptive input. The accompanying manual provides excellent information on the significance of the observations reported in the questionnaire.

Morton and Wolford also have published an excellent questionnaire titled, "Analysis of Sensory Behaviour Inventory" (1994). It reviews all of the sensory systems and is divided into observations that may suggest sensory-seeking versus sensory-avoidant behaviours. It includes a method to organize your observations and a worksheet to help summarize your observations, discuss implications, and note recommendations.

Dunn (1994) developed the "Sensory Profile," which has 125 behavioural statements that are organized into all the sensory systems and includes observations about activity level and emotional and social behaviours. This is the questionnaire that was recently used to compare the performance of children with and without autism, which indicated that 85% of the items differentiated between the sensory processing abilities of children with autism from those children without autism (Kientz and Dunn, 1997).

Another useful tool is the "Durrand Motivation Assessment Scale" (1988). This scale looks at types of unusual behaviour and helps to analyze what motivates the behaviour. Questions about the behaviour are presented, and the answers help to understand if the behaviour is motivated by a sensory need, the need for attention, the need to avoid or escape, or an attempt to communicate the wish for a desired item or action.

Sensory Screening

Vestibular System

Does your child

- ❏ Appear fearful of playground equipment or carnival rides?
- ❏ Become sick easily in cars, elevators, or rides?
- ❏ Appear fearful of heights or stair climbing?
- ❏ Avoid balancing activities?
- ❏ Seek fast-moving activities?
- ❏ Avoid participation in sports or active games?
- ❏ Seem oblivious to risks of heights and moving equipment?
- ❏ Engage in frequent spinning, jumping, bouncing, or running?

Tactile System

Does your child

- ❏ Avoid touch or contact?
- ❏ Dislike and avoid messy play?
- ❏ Appear irritated by certain clothing or food textures?
- ❏ Appear irritated when someone is in close proximity?
- ❏ Often appear very active or fidgety?
- ❏ Have difficulty manipulating small objects?
- ❏ Use his or her hands to explore objects?
- ❏ Mouth objects?

Proprioceptive System

Does your child

- ❏ Exert too much, or not enough, pressure when handling objects?
- ❏ Assume body positions necessary to perform different tasks?
- ❏ Enjoy rough and tumble play?
- ❏ Seek deep-pressure by squeezing between furniture?
- ❏ Relax when given firm massages?

Visual System

Does your child

- ❏ Appear uncomfortable in strong sunlight?
- ❏ Appear sensitive to changes in lighting?

…continues

- ❏ Turn away from television or computer screens?
- ❏ Focus on shadows, reflections, or spinning objects?
- ❏ Have difficulty scanning the environment?
- ❏ Respond when new people enter a room?

Auditory System

Does your child

- ❏ Become upset with loud or unexpected noises?
- ❏ Hum or sing to screen out unwanted noise?
- ❏ Respond to voices?

Olfactory (Smell) and Gustatory (Taste) Systems

Does your child

- ❏ Dislike strong smells or tastes?
- ❏ Crave strong smells or tastes?
- ❏ Smear his or her feces?
- ❏ Eat non-edible items?

Indentifying Difficulties in Self-Care Skills

Self-Care Checklist

Touch

❑ Has difficulty tolerating touch by a facecloth/towel

❑ Rubs the spot that was touched

❑ Needs rigid rituals

❑ Has difficulty tolerating splashing in the bathtub

❑ Dislikes teeth brushing

❑ Complains that the toothbrush/hairbrush hurts him or her

❑ Reacts aggressively to touch

❑ Dislikes hair brushing or anything on the head

❑ Dislikes touch to his or her bottom from a diaper or toilet paper

❑ Wants to wear clothes all the time or may prefer to be naked

❑ Has difficulty tolerating temperature change

Proprioception

❑ Drops objects constantly (toothpaste, brush, etc.)

❑ Exerts too much or not enough pressure with objects (e.g., squeezes the toothpaste so tightly that too much comes out, or the child is unable to take the cap off)

❑ Really enjoys the shower, rough towelling, or firm hair brushing

❑ Is unable to change body position to accommodate task (e.g., lean head back to rinse shampoo)

Vestibular

❑ Resists change in head position/movement (e.g., hair brushing or shampooing)

❑ Prefers to hold head upright

❑ Becomes disoriented after a change in head position

❑ Has difficulty with balance getting in and out of the tub, washing lower body

❑ Has difficulty bending over the sink, fearful of sitting on the toilet—especially if feet are off the ground

Visual

❑ Has difficulty scanning the environment for desired object

❑ Has difficulty guiding movement when using a mirror

❑ Is fascinated with bubbles, dripping water

❑ Has difficulty tolerating the reflection of light off the water or shiny sink

...continues

Auditory

- ❏ Becomes upset by loud noises (e.g., toilet flushing, water running, hairdryer)
- ❏ Enjoys loud sounds and repeats them again and again (e.g., flushing the toilet)
- ❏ Hums or sings to screen incoming auditory input
- ❏ Is easily distracted by noises
- ❏ Covers ears with hands to screen the loud, hollow sound of the bathroom
- ❏ Has to do self-care skills outside the bathroom because the reflected sound is intolerable

Smell/Taste

- ❏ Has poor tolerance of perfumes
- ❏ Has difficulty tolerating toothpaste
- ❏ Craves strong tastes; eats toothpaste, soap, shampoo
- ❏ Does not seem to smell even very strong smells
- ❏ Smears feces
- ❏ Holds nose or gags during self-care activities

General Observations

Activity Level

- ❏ Is sedentary; prefers sitting tasks
- ❏ Has difficulty staying still
- ❏ Has difficulty staying in place long enough to participate in school activities
- ❏ Is fidgety
- ❏ Has strong desire for movement breaks
- ❏ Shifts position constantly during seated activity

Emotional

- ❏ Has poor self-esteem
- ❏ Requires more preparation and support
- ❏ Seems behaviourally immature
- ❏ Is overly sensitive to criticism
- ❏ Does not exhibiti understanding of a concept in the performance of tasks
- ❏ Is fearful, anxious
- ❏ Has difficulty with transitions
- ❏ Is rigid, stubborn, and controlling in effort to compensate for poor planning skills
- ❏ Has temper tantrums often
- ❏ Is easily frustrated
- ❏ Has difficulty sleeping
- ❏ Has difficulty recognizing and labelling the feeling of being out of control
- ❏ Has difficulty self-calming
- ❏ Has difficulty interacting and making friends

Dressing Checklist

Touch

- ❏ Dislikes rigid clothing (e.g., jeans), bindings on clothing (e.g., waistband, wrist, cuffs)
- ❏ Strongly likes/dislikes tight clothing/nakedness/shoes and socks
- ❏ Dislikes dressing; opposes changing clothing
- ❏ Has difficulty with seasonal changes or changes due to weather
- ❏ Has a very narrow range of clothing items that can be tolerated
- ❏ Dislikes undergarments; usually prefers to wear them inside out
- ❏ Pulls at hats, mittens
- ❏ Constantly pulls or rubs clothing
- ❏ Hates new clothes
- ❏ Needs all tags cut out
- ❏ Has difficulty choosing clothing; dressing is often very stressful

Proprioception

- ❏ Constantly dropping of items from the hand (e.g., belt, pants when being pulled up); easily tires while dressing
- ❏ Has difficulty placing the body appropriately in relation to the clothing (e.g., leg in the leg hole)
- ❏ Problems with the finesse of dressing (e.g., ensuring the shirt is tucked in, the zipper is up)
- ❏ Does not seem to notice when clothing is twisted on body

Vestibular

- ❏ Has difficulty maintaining balance during dressing, especially when bending over to put legs into pants or socks
- ❏ Loses orientation when the head is moved (e.g., to look down to put on shoes)
- ❏ Has difficulty maintaining attention because the need to balance takes up so much energy
- ❏ Tendency to rush through the activity to avoid losing balance
- ❏ Craves movement during dressing
- ❏ Fatigues easily

Visual

- ❏ Has difficulty finding clothing in closet and drawer
- ❏ Has difficulty matching socks and shoes
- ❏ Is distracted by patterns; may prefer a solid colour
- ❏ Has difficulty finding buttons or zipper on a garment
- ❏ Has difficulty matching button to buttonhole
- ❏ Has difficulty using vision to guide movement
- ❏ Has difficulty with balance

...continues

Auditory

❑   Has difficulty with clothing that makes noise when body moves

❑   Is easily distracted by noise during dressing

❑   Has difficulty hearing verbal prompts during dressing

Smell/Taste

❑   Does not wear new clothing because of smell

❑   Prefers clothing to be washed and dried with non-perfumed detergents/fabric softeners

❑   Has poor tolerance of decals or iron-ons due to smell

❑   Dislikes freshly ironed clothing because the heat from the iron can bring out smell

Eating Checklist

Touch

- ❏ Prefers food of consistent texture and temperature
- ❏ Dislikes "surprise" texture in foods (e.g., noodle in soup)
- ❏ Frequently gags when texture of food is changed
- ❏ Eats very limited diet due to sensory restrictions
- ❏ Has difficulty tolerating utensils in the mouth; prefers to eat finger foods
- ❏ Frequently drinks during eating to wash food out of the mouth
- ❏ Does not feel food on face or may be excessively neat
- ❏ Only uses finger tips when eating; difficulty tolerating touch to the inside of the hand
- ❏ Is a picky eater
- ❏ Has poor awareness of pain and temperature in the mouth or decreased sensation that could lead to choking

Proprioception

- ❏ Prefers chewy or crunchy foods to increase sensory input (e.g., fruit chews or chips)
- ❏ Does not appropriately chew food (could lead to choking)
- ❏ Easily tires, especially during meals that require chewing
- ❏ Does not use enough force to bite an apple, cut meat, etc.
- ❏ Props body up, uses hand under chin, or leans head on arm or body against table to stabilize for eating

Vestibular

- ❏ Has difficulty with sitting balance
- ❏ Has difficulty maintaining attention to the task when the head position changes to accommodate the fork/spoon
- ❏ Needs movement; frequently stands up and sits down
- ❏ Constantly shifts position in the chair
- ❏ Tires easily

Visual

- ❏ Has difficulty guiding movement with the eyes
- ❏ Has difficulty finding the food or cutlery against a patterned tablecloth
- ❏ Is bothered by patterns on the table or plate
- ❏ Is distracted by visual input
- ❏ Hangs head close to food to block out extra visual input

... continues

Auditory

- ❑ Is distracted by the noise of the food, utensils, people talking
- ❑ Dislikes the sound inside his head while chewing
- ❑ Has difficulty eating when someone else is eating or talking
- ❑ Appears not to hear, even when called

Smell/Taste

- ❑ Gags easily; has difficulty with strong tastes/odors
- ❑ Tolerates a narrow range of foods
- ❑ Exhibits pica (chewing and eating non-edible items)
- ❑ Shows hesitantation to try new foods
- ❑ Is a poor eater
- ❑ Becomes upset with the smell of food as it is cooking
- ❑ Shows strong preferences for some foods; wants to eat them at every meal
- ❑ Seems not to smell; not motivated to eat because there is no taste

School/Work Checklist

Touch

- ❑ Avoids expression of affection, such as hugs and pats by teacher or peers
- ❑ Has difficulty tolerating touch by others; poor ability to stand in line, sit in a small circle, or work in a confined space with others
- ❑ Dislikes holding writing or cutting utensils in the hand
- ❑ Dislikes holding the job's tools-of-the-trade
- ❑ Dislikes touch on hand by glue, paint, stickers, tape, or objects that are wet and/or dirty
- ❑ Has difficulty tolerating close one-on-one instruction and hand-over-hand demonstration
- ❑ Tends to use the mouth, not the hands, to learn about toys and other objects
- ❑ Uses minimal touch when working on a keyboard
- ❑ Touches objects or people excessively
- ❑ Reacts aggressively to touch by others
- ❑ Has outbursts during lining-up or circle time

Proprioception

- ❑ Has trouble staying in one place and likes to take frequent movement breaks
- ❑ Stabilizes self against the furniture; (e.g., may "hook" arm around a chair to stay upright)
- ❑ "Locks" joints to maintain posture
- ❑ Seems to prop the body up
- ❑ Has weak grasp
- ❑ Has difficulty accommodating to changes in the environment (e.g., has a great deal of difficulty when the classroom has been re-organized)
- ❑ Frequently drops books, pencils, hammer, dishcloth, chalk, etc.
- ❑ Tires easily
- ❑ Uses a chewing strategy to maintain attention and focus
- ❑ Uses a self-stimulatory behaviour to maintain attention or relieve stress

Vestibular

- ❑ Is distractible and loses visual attention easily, especially if the head is moved
- ❑ Uses a self-stimulatory behaviour with the head in order to maintain attention
- ❑ Has difficulty with visual tracking; easily loses place
- ❑ Needs to take frequent movement breaks
- ❑ Has poor balance in chairs, on floor, and while changing the body's position
- ❑ Fears and avoids the playground, gym, and stairs
- ❑ Takes unnecessary risks on the playground and in the gym
- ❑ Dislikes the car/bus ride
- ❑ Dislikes stops/starts, going backward, or changing direction in the car/bus   *... continues*

Visual

- ❑ Has difficulty finding objects against a cluttered background
- ❑ Is unable to visually scan across a page without losing the sentence
- ❑ Often loses place when reading
- ❑ Is interested in visually stimulating objects and will create visual stims by spinning or dropping objects
- ❑ Pays attention to detail but fails to see the whole
- ❑ Has strong visual memory
- ❑ Has trouble staying between the lines when colouring or writing
- ❑ Squints
- ❑ Has difficulty putting puzzles together
- ❑ Is uncomfortable in very light settings; prefers the dark
- ❑ Looks intently at people/objects
- ❑ Hesitates going up or down stairs
- ❑ Gets lost easily

Auditory

- ❑ Covers ears frequently
- ❑ Does not respond when name is called
- ❑ Speaks in a loud voice to screen out incoming noise
- ❑ Startles to loud noises (e.g., PA system, door banging)
- ❑ Is distracted by noise or is intolerant of background noise
- ❑ Is very sensitive to noises from other sources (e.g., the next classroom)
- ❑ Prefers activities that enable screening of auditory input (e.g., tearing paper, opening and closing the door, humming to self)

Smell/Taste

- ❑ Exhibits excessive need to smell items or people
- ❑ Dislikes cleaning days because everything smells like cleanser
- ❑ Reacts negatively when people wear new smells, or seems to lose interest in the person when the smell is different
- ❑ Has many allergies
- ❑ Displays a very small personal space as proximity is needed to smell someone
- ❑ Is hyposensitive to taste and may snack on crayons or chalk (safety issue)

Play Checklist

Touch

- ❏ Touches objects or people excessively
- ❏ Has rigid, controlling personality
- ❏ Dislikes getting messy
- ❏ Does not use the whole hand; prefers to use fingertips
- ❏ Reacts aggressively to touch by others
- ❏ Shows decreased awareness of pain and temperature
- ❏ Mouths objects if hands are overly sensitive
- ❏ Has a strong preference for certain textures in toys
- ❏ Chooses predictable toys to prevent surprises
- ❏ Prefers dry to wet/dirty play
- ❏ Uses toys differently than intended—may use them for a sensory purpose, rather than for play

Proprioception

- ❏ Prefers gross motor toys to manipulatives because of the full body motion
- ❏ Seems to have weak muscles
- ❏ Tires easily
- ❏ Has a weak grasp
- ❏ Seems accident-prone
- ❏ Seems to enjoy falling and crashing
- ❏ Does not easily change body position in relation to the toy
- ❏ Drops pieces of a toy or uses excessive (or not enough) force when playing with the toy
- ❏ Does not play with the toy appropriately; uses it for a sensory purpose
- ❏ Chews on toys to increase attention and/or postural stability
- ❏ "Locks" joints in order to maintain position
- ❏ Has poor endurance
- ❏ Prefers sedentary activities

Vestibular

- ❏ Becomes fearful when feet leave the ground
- ❏ Dislikes being upside down
- ❏ Avoids playground activities
- ❏ Avoids play activities that call for movement
- ❏ Has an excessive need for movement
- ❏ Has difficulty adjusting the body to prepare for changes in position   *... continues*

- ❏ Creates self-movement through rocking or constant shifting in a chair
- ❏ Uses eyes to compensate for balance difficulties
- ❏ Takes unnecessary risks

Visual

- ❏ Has an excessive interest in moving, spinning, or patterned movements
- ❏ Has difficulty putting puzzles together
- ❏ Is uncomfortable in bright light—prefers the dark
- ❏ Concentrates on details and is unable to see the "whole picture"
- ❏ Loses place when reading
- ❏ Has difficulty visually tracking or finding an object within a busy background
- ❏ Gets lost easily
- ❏ Has trouble matching and sorting objects
- ❏ Hesitates going up or down steps

Auditory

- ❏ Is defensive about sounds (may cover ears)
- ❏ Startles easily with loud, unexpected noises
- ❏ Is fascinated by certain sounds and repeats them often
- ❏ Constantly makes sound to block out other sounds
- ❏ Stops playing in the presence of unfamiliar sounds
- ❏ Is easily distracted by sounds
- ❏ Seems not to be a part of social play

Smell/Taste

- ❏ Smells or tastes toys prior to play
- ❏ Dislikes new toys or toys with a strong smell

Social Skills Checklist

Touch

- ❑ Isolates himself from touch by others
- ❑ Dislikes crowds and groups of children for fear of being bumped
- ❑ Reacts aggressively when bumped or touched by others
- ❑ Has difficulty tolerating hugs, kisses, and signs of affection
- ❑ Is unable to play with others due to the proximity of the other children
- ❑ Has difficulty working alongside others if space is too small
- ❑ Seeks out deep-pressure and frequently bumps into others
- ❑ Is self-injurious
- ❑ Touches objects and people excessively
- ❑ Has a rigid and controlling personality

Proprioception

- ❑ Plays rough in effort to gain more input
- ❑ Seeks out deep-pressure, hugs
- ❑ Squeezes self into small places (e.g., between the sofa and the wall instead of on the sofa)
- ❑ Exerts too much (or not enough) pressure when giving a handshake
- ❑ Claps, crashes, or bangs head excessively
- ❑ Is self-injurious

Vestibular

- ❑ Craves or avoids movement (depending on the ability to process vestibular input)
- ❑ Turns whole body to look at you
- ❑ Has difficulty approaching and standing/sitting near someone due to immature balance
- ❑ Becomes dizzy watching other children move around
- ❑ Becomes excited or anxious in an environment full of movement

Visual

- ❑ Has difficulty reading facial expression/social cues
- ❑ Is more comfortable in the dark
- ❑ Looks intensely at objects/people
- ❑ Has difficulty visually scanning to find friends
- ❑ Has difficulty locating and keeping friends in the visual field, especially in a busy environment
- ❑ Has poor eye contact; may find eye contact very stressful
- ❑ Stares off into space

... continues

- ❑ Does not use eyes to guide movement
- ❑ Cannot process or tolerate extremes of intensity and colour
- ❑ Squints

Auditory

- ❑ Appears not to hear, even if own name is called
- ❑ Is oversensitive to the sounds of others
- ❑ Constantly hums or sings to drown out environmental noise
- ❑ Dislikes crowds and noisy places
- ❑ Covers ears

Smell/Taste

- ❑ Overreacts to new people, new scents
- ❑ Uses a small personal space in effort to smell another person
- ❑ Licks others in order to interact

Chapter 5

Strategies for Managing Challenging Behaviour

The first step in managing challenging behaviours in children with PDD is to understand the reason behind the observed behaviour. Williamson (1996) identifies many factors affecting behaviour in young children with PDD, including the physical environment, the child's current emotional state, availability of a caregiver, general level of arousal, and accumulated negative reactions to sensory build up. Certain behaviours may reflect a child's response to an inefficient nervous system that might not be able to accurately register, orient, or interpret sensory information.

Children with PDD can act as a barometer, reflecting the emotional states of others. Greater understanding can prevent negative responses to the behaviours these children sometimes exhibit. The theory of sensory integration, as presented in chapters 2 and 3, can help you better understand some of these behaviours. Chapter 4 provided tools to help determine if a child is experiencing a problem with sensory integration.

The second step is preventing the occurrence of problem behaviours. Strategies based on sensory integration theory can accommodate sensory needs and help prevent some inappropriate behaviours. These strategies include the implementation of a sensory diet and use of the Wilbarger Protocol.

The third step to managing challenging behaviours is to develop consistent procedures to employ when the behaviour occurs. This chapter describes some very specific problem behaviours and offers strategies to implement when the behaviour occurs. It also provides some general calming and alerting ideas. These strategies are most helpful for those children who have been identified as having sensory-related problems. It is not always clear why certain behaviours occur. Sometimes what begins as a particular behaviour to cope with a sensory need develops into a habit or a learned pattern of response. Sometimes a traditional behavioural approach needs to be used alone or in conjunction with a sensory integration approach. Some behaviours that may appear related to sensory-motor needs may be involuntary tics or reflections of other neurological problems.

You can teach children to recognize and understand their own sensory needs and then give them strategies to increase attention, decrease stress, and improve reactions to sensory stimulation. Many of the strategies presented throughout this book can easily be taught to children. At the end of this chapter is a program that has been adapted to teach relaxation techniques to children with PDD. This chapter includes the following topics

1. The Wilbarger Protocol for Sensory Defensiveness
2. Sensory Diets
3. General Calming and Alerting Strategies
4. Strategies for Specific Problems
5. A Relaxation Technique for Children

1. The Wilbarger Protocol for Sensory Defensiveness

The Wilbarger Protocol (Wilbarger, 1991) is a specific, professionally guided treatment regime designed to reduce sensory defensiveness. The Wilbarger Protocol has its origins in sensory integration theory, and it has evolved through clinical use. It involves deep-touch pressure throughout the day. Patricia Wilbarger, M.Ed., OTR, FAOTA, an internationally recognized expert who specializes in the assessment and treatment of sensory defensiveness, developed this technique.

Ms. Wilbarger offers training courses where professionals can learn how to administer her technique and has produced videotapes, audiotapes, and other publications (see Resources). At these courses, she also shares strategies for integrating the protocol into intervention plans and training parents, teachers, and other caregivers.

There currently is a lack of documented research to substantiate this technique. However, the protocol has been used by many occupational therapists who have noted positive results with a variety of populations. Many parents of children with autism have reported that their children have responded positively to this technique, including reduction in sensory defensiveness, as well as improved behaviour and interaction. Many adults with autism have also reported reduction in sensory defensiveness, decreased anxiety, and increased comfort in the environment through the use of this technique. We have observed significant behavioural changes in many of our clients following the introduction of the Wilbarger Protocol.

The Wilbarger Protocol represents one of those difficulties in clinical practice where positive results are observed in treatment regimes that have not yet been fully validated by scientific research. However, because of the strength of anecdotal reporting and our own observations, we feel we would be doing a disservice if we did not advise our clients about this technique. When we discuss this option with our clients, we review why it is being recommended and provide them with information on sensory defensiveness. We also inform them about the absence of research in this area, and we make it clear that it is their decision if they want to include the technique in their treatment regimes.

An occupational therapist who has been trained to use the technique, and who knows sensory integration theory, needs to teach and supervise the Wilbarger Protocol. This statement cannot be emphasized enough. If the technique is carried out without proper instruction, it could be uncomfortable for the child and may lead to undesired results.

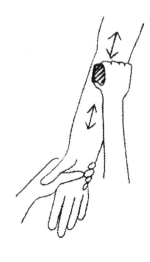

The first step of the Wilbarger Protocol involves providing deep pressure to the skin on the arms, back, and legs through the use of a special surgical brush. Many people mistakenly call this technique "brushing" because a surgical brush is used. The term "brushing" does not adequately reflect the amount of pressure that is exerted against the skin with the movement of the brush. A more appropriate analogy would be that it is like giving someone a deep massage using a surgical brush. The use of the brush in a slow and methodical manner provides consistent deep-pressure input to a wide area of the skin surface on the body. Ms. Wilbarger has found and has recommended a specific surgical brush to be most effective. The face and stomach are never brushed.

Following the "massage" stage, the child receives gentle compressions to the shoulders, elbows, wrists/fingers, hips, knees/ankles, and sternum. These compressions provide substantial proprioceptive input. Ms. Wilbarger feels that it is critical that joint compressions follow the use of the surgical brush, and if there is no time to complete both steps, then compressions should not be administered.

The complete routine should only take about three minutes. This technique can be incorporated into a sensory diet schedule. The procedure is initially repeated every ninety minutes. After a period of time, the frequency is reduced. Eventually the procedure can be stopped, but gains can be maintained. Some children immediately enjoy this input, and others resist the first few sessions. You may distract the child by singing or offering a mouth or fidget toy.

Some children really like the administration of this protocol and will seek out the brush and bring it to their parents, teachers, or caregivers. Other children tolerate it with little reaction, and occasionally a child is resistive. If the child continues to resist, and you see negative changes, you must reconsider the use of the technique and contact the supervising therapist. This has rarely occurred in our practices.

Case Studies

As you will see in the following case reports of children who are in our practices, the results of using the Wilbarger Protocol sometimes can be very dramatic. At other times, although the changes have not been as dramatic and have occurred over a longer period of time, they have been significant in positively changing the lives of the children and their families.

Pat

> *Pat is a four-year-old boy who has a diagnosis of autism. His occupational therapist concluded that he had sensory defensiveness. Pat was particularly reactive to light touch and unexpected or loud noises. He was very uncomfortable in settings with lots of people and activity. In these environments, Pat became very anxious and would run around the perimeter of the room or setting that he was in. This could be quite dangerous in parking lots where Pat would attempt to run, and his parents had to hold him securely. It also presented as a problem when his parents took him shopping or to family gatherings.*

The Wilbarger Protocol was recommended as part of an intervention plan that also included a variety of prescribed sensory activities throughout the day. After only one week, Pat's parents noted a significant decrease in his level of anxiety and his running behaviours. After one month, it became much easier to take Pat shopping and to family gatherings. He even became more willing to interact with his peers and unfamiliar adults!

Amy

Amy is a six-year-old girl who has a diagnosis of autism. Her occupational therapist concluded that she had sensory defensiveness. Amy avoided light touch, was uncomfortable with many clothing textures, and resisted many self-care routines, including face washing, tooth brushing, hair washing, and hair brushing. Amy's hair was the biggest battle for Amy's parents, and the babysitter and Amy often would cry for long periods of time after hair brushing.

The Wilbarger Protocol was recommended as part of an intervention plan. The Protocol was started over the weekend, and no other intervention was provided during that time.

Amy's babysitter came to work on Monday morning and did not know that the Protocol was being considered or that it had been initiated. She babysat Amy during the day and was responsible for her self-care routines. When Amy's parents came home from work that day, her babysitter reported that Amy did not resist hair brushing and was more comfortable with washing routines. She asked Amy's parents if they had started giving her medication over the weekend!

Reducing Hypersensitivity in the Mouth

Patricia Wilbarger has also developed a specialized program to help reduce hypersensitivity in the mouth. This type of sensitivity, sometimes called oral defensiveness, can result in limited food choices and can interfere with tooth brushing and face washing. This technique involves use of the thumb to apply pressure along the base of the upper teeth (a surgical glove may be used).

The pressure should be similar to the amount of pressure used when rubbing an eyelid. Following the sweeping motions, gentle downward pressure is applied to the lower jaw by placing fingers over the middle of the lower teeth and pressing down.

2. Sensory Diet

A sensory diet is a planned and scheduled activity program designed to meet a child's specific sensory needs. Wilbarger and Wilbarger (1991) developed the approach to provide the "just right" combination of sensory input to achieve and maintain optimal levels of arousal and performance in the nervous system. The ability to appropriately orient and respond to sensations can be enhanced by a proper sensory diet. A sensory diet also helps reduce protective or sensory defensive responses that can negatively affect social contact and interaction.

There are certain types of sensory activities that are similar to eating a "main course" and are very powerful and satisfying. These activities provide movement, deep-touch pressure, and heavy work. They are the powerhouses of any sensory diet, as they have the most significant and long-lasting impact on the nervous system (Wilbarger, 1995; Hanschu, 1997).

There are other types of activities that may be beneficial, but their impact is not as great. These "sensory snacks," or "mood makers," are activities that last a shorter period of time and generally include mouth, auditory, visual, or smell experiences.

A sensory diet is not simply indiscriminately adding more sensory stimulation into the child's day. Additional stimulation can sometimes intensify negative responses. The most successful sensory diets include activities where the child is an active participant. Every child has unique sensory needs, and his sensory diet must be customized for individual needs and responses. An occupational therapist needs to evaluate sensory processing abilities and determine what types of sensory activities would be beneficial.

The sensory diet can be a powerful behavioural tool. If the sensory diet is properly designed and implemented, it can help prevent many challenging behaviours, including self-stimulatory and self-abusive behaviours. Engaging children in sensory experiences on a regular schedule can help them focus, attend, and interact. Children can feel less anxious when they feel more comfortable and in control.

One of the main aims of the sensory diet is to prevent sensory and emotional overload by satisfying the nervous system's sensory needs. However, it can also be used as a recovery technique. Knowing the child's sensory needs (or sensory profile) and calming activities can be of great assistance when the child becomes overwhelmed and out-of-control. Adults need to be taught to take prompt action if they see the child becoming overwhelmed or are approaching what some parents call a "meltdown."

Common indicators that a child's sensory processing system needs help include silliness, giddiness, noise making, aimless running, or pacing. These behaviours may intensify into repetitive stereotypic behaviours, including self-injury. Sometimes the child will simply "shut down," becoming passive, sleepy, or self-absorbed.

There are many ways to implement a sensory diet at home and in the classroom, but it takes commitment on the part of the whole team. Depending on the needs of the child, a sensory diet can be comprised of very specific activities carried out at prescribed times. The following form allows you to list specific times to provide activities, as well as methods to compensate for sensory problems during self-care routines.

For children with PDD, the use of visual aids (pictures and words) is helpful to ensure that the children understand their daily routines and can anticipate when they will be engaging in certain activities. Sensory diet activities can easily be incorporated into visual schedules and choice boards. A clear beginning and end to all activities is necessary.

A poster hung in a classroom or at home can have pictures that represent regular daily activities. When completed, put the picture in an envelope marked DONE. This type of visual system can help all children, as it adds a sense of order and predictability to the class or home environment.

Sensory Diet / Accomodations

Name: _____   Date: _____

Time	Daily Events	Activities/Accommodations	Comments
	Wake-Up		
	Self-Care		
	Breakfast		
	Arrival at School or Childcare		
	Mid-Morning		
	Lunch		
	Mid-Afternoon		
	Arrival Home		
	Dinner		
	Evening Activity		
	Self-Care		
	Bedtime		

A Sample Preschool Sensory Diet

This sensory diet was established for Philip, a hyperactive, four-year-old boy with little verbal language. He was also sensory defensive to touch and sound. He attended his community daycare every day. Recommendations included both highly prescribed suggestions (relaxation techniques at start of day and Wilbarger Protocol every 90 minutes) and a list of activities that Philip should be offered on a regular basis.

Recommendations

Progressive relaxation exercises (in this chapter) started Philip's day to assist with transition to the daycare setting

The Wilbarger Protocol was provided every 90 minutes to address the touch and sound sensitivities.

Free-play activities were chosen from the following list

- ❑ Mini-trampoline, jumping on an old mattress; Sit 'n Spin, rocking boat, swinging, jumping on cushions, "diving" into big box or futon, lie on him and make a "hot dog," jumping into sand or snow
- ❑ Hop balls (on soft surfaces)—try making them into "chairs" by turning them with the handle down and then stabilizing ball beside the wall, in a corner, or in an inner tube
- ❑ Regular climbing toys, slides, tunnels, big blocks
- ❑ Balance beams
- ❑ Obstacle courses for planning movement
- ❑ Running or running errands (e.g., "Run to the sandbox and bring the yellow truck.")
- ❑ Jumping jacks
- ❑ Wall push-ups (stand in a door frame and "push-out" the sides)
- ❑ Filling a large pot with water, lifting/carrying it, and dumping it out
- ❑ Swinging across monkey bars, hanging from your hands
- ❑ Bikes and riding toys–provide a destination by allowing "crashes" into a soft, big ball or beanbag

Tactile Activities

- ❑ Daily access to dry sensory play materials (e.g., rice, sand, or beans)
- ❑ Toys hidden in sensory play materials
- ❑ "High fives" through out day!!
- ❑ Drawing in sand or salt
- ❑ Therapy tubing or band to pull on, therapy putty, koosh balls, balloons, or rubber gloves filled with things like corn, rice, flour, etc.
- ❑ Hand massage
- ❑ Wheelbarrow walking over various floor surfaces

Sitting/Circle Time Ideas

❑ Deep pressure to his back and hips while he sits in circle time

❑ Weighted vest (instructions on how to make a weighted vest can be found in chapter 9)

❑ Fidget toys to hold quietly while listening (e.g., "stress" ball, vibrating pen, Tangle Toy®)

❑ Assuming more challenging positions (e.g., high kneel, on tummy, half kneel, etc.)

❑ Sitting in padded chair or beanbag chair, sitting in staff's lap, sitting against body pillow, "move 'n sit" cushion

❑ Any musical toy (e.g., kazoo, harmonica, party blowers, etc.) that requires breath support

❑ Defined "spot" for each child—using laundry basket, carpet square, or something similar

Observed Changes as a Result of the Sensory Diet

Philip began to enjoy attending daycare as his anxiety and need for uncontrolled movement decreased. He became calmer and made transitions easier. At home he stopped complaining when brushing his teeth and would wash his own face and hands. He would seek out his sensory "pictures" to request a specific activity such as playing on the big ball. Many of the activities that were included in Philip's sensory diet were activities that were already part of the classroom routine. Therefore, his classmates happily joined Philip for many activities. He soon was better able to interact with his peers as his discomfort with having the children near him decreased.

3. General Calming, Organizing, and Alerting Techniques

The following list provides methods that can help calm, organize, or alert the nervous system. The list must be only used as a general guideline, as activities that calm one child may be alerting to another. These strategies can be incorporated into a sensory diet, or they may help deal with a specific situation.

Calming Techniques

Sensory soothing or calming experiences can help any child who is anxious, but they are particularly useful for children who are sensory defensive. They help to relax the nervous system and can reduce exaggerated responses to sensory input.

- Warm or tepid bath
- Deep-pressure massage; backrub using comfort touch
- Joint compressions
- Stretches
- Snuggling in a sleeping bag, beanbag chair, or large pillows
- Blanket wrap (neutral warmth) or swaddling for a younger child
- Firm pressure and skin-to-skin contact
- Slow rocking or swaying—rocking chair, in adult's lap or arms, on tummy in a head-to-heel direction (rhythmic motion)
- Slow swinging back and forth in a blanket
- Lycra/spandex clothing
- Neoprene vest
- Weighted vest or collar
- Lap "snake" (instructions for making a lap snake are in chapter 9)
- Lavender, vanilla, banana, or other soothing smells
- Sucking
- Hideout, fort, or quiet corner
- Fidget toys
- Progressive muscle relaxation
- White noise or quiet music with a steady beat
- Bear hugs (child faces away from you)
- Hugging a teddy bear, giving self-hugs
- Finger hugs and tugs
- Reduced noise and light levels (turn off the TV, radio, and lights)

Organizing Techniques

Organizing experiences can help a child who is either over- or under-active become focused and attentive.

- Sucking a pacifier or hard candy or using curly straws
- Vibration—use a vibrating pillow, battery vibrating wiggle pen, toy massager
- Proprioceptive activities (see list in chapter 8) especially hanging, pushing, pulling, or lifting heavy objects
- Chewing, blowing (see oral motor activity list in chapter 8)
- Swimming
- Adding rhythm to the activity

Alerting Techniques

Alerting experiences can help a child who is under-reactive to sensory input, passive, or lethargic become more focused and attentive. It is important to determine if the child is in a "shutdown" mode in response to sensory defensiveness. If this is the case, alerting strategies should not be used. Alerting activities need to be closely monitored to prevent over stimulation.

- Bright lighting and fresh, cool air
- Fast swinging
- Quick unpredictable movement (bouncing on a ball, lap, or mini-trampoline)
- Drinking ice water or carbonated drink
- Cold water play
- Running–tag games, hide 'n seek, errands
- Sitting on a ball chair, water mat, or air pillow
- Misting cool water from spray bottle on face
- Loud, fast music and sudden noises
- Cause and effect toys with sounds and lights
- Strong odours (e.g., perfume, peppermint, etc.)
- Visually stimulating rooms

4. Strategies for Specific Problem Behaviours

In the following section, we will present some approaches to commonly seen behaviours. The purpose of certain behaviours may be to seek sensory input or avoid sensory input. Strategies for specific behaviours related to self-care routines (problems with food texture, hair cutting, etc.) are included in chapter 7.

Sensory-Seeking Behaviours

Many children with PDD crave sensory input and seem to have an insatiable need for certain types of stimulation. The motto for sensory input, "feed the need," is generally good advice. However, there are times when sensory-seeking behaviours may not provide the most organizing, calming, or socially acceptable input. It is appropriate to redirect behaviour, always striving to provide the appropriate input in the most socially acceptable manner.

Biting and Teeth Grinding

Why?

The child may be hyposensitive to this input and probably has no idea that he is actually hurting himself. Teeth grinding may be used as a calming strategy. It's also seen in children with poor balance, perhaps in an effort to stabilize themselves.

Try:

Sensory diet with appropriate opportunities for strong sensory input to jaw muscles and oral and tactile discrimination experiences. Children may enjoy chewing on beverage tubing to alleviate stress and calm their nervous system. Whatever strategy is used, it will be most effective if used in all settings. The child will then be able to generalize the coping strategy.

Look for the circumstances prior to the biting sometimes sometimes. If the root of the aggressive behaviour is sensory defensiveness to sound, touch, or movement, try to identify the sensitivity and eliminate it (or position the child to minimize exposure to this noxious sensory input). Warn the child and teach coping strategies. Use the Wilbarger Protocol to reduce sensory defensiveness.

Another oral pressure technique to try: place the flats of index and middle fingers against the space between the upper lip and nose and press gently, but firmly, so that the child is receiving deep pressure.

Running, Spinning, or Other Movement

Why?

Running, spinning, and other movements provide strong vestibular and proprioceptive stimulation.

Try:

Sensory diet with appropriate opportunities for strong vestibular and proprioceptive input. Preschoolers love to play tag or "Come and Get Me;" older children can run around the track, do relay races, rollerblade, or find alternative ways to get that vestibular "fix" (see chapter 8).

Crashing, Bumping, and Clinging

Why?

These activities provide soothing proprioceptive, vestibular, and deep-pressure touch input. If the child has a high pain tolerance, he or she may actually need a very strong stimulus just to register some sensation. Ear infections should also be ruled out as a source of pain because a child may be unable to localize the source.

Try:

Address the source of pain. If it is an ear infection or other medical condition, send the child to his doctor for treatment. Use the Wilbarger Protocol to reduce sensory defensiveness. If the child bangs his head, make a weighted hat or bike helmet for calming.

Hitting, Slapping, Pinching, Squeezing, Grabbing, and Pulling

Why?

The hand may be extremely sensitive compared to other body parts, and sensory input in the palm may help to override the painful response to light touch.

Try:

Use the Wilbarger Protocol to reduce sensory defensiveness. Learn alternate means for obtaining some deep-pressure/heavy muscle work. For example, a child may push/pull on the seat of his desk chair, press very hard into the desk top, press hands together, or hand massage. Ask your OT for appropriate exercises or fidget bag toys (see chapter 9), gadgets that your child can have with him to keep hands occupied. Experiment with a Bungee cord bracelet (see chapter 9) or other wrist-bands and watchbands that provide pressure. Toys that offer vibration may also be helpful.

Playing with Saliva

Why?

This provides tactile input to the mouth, fingers, and the spot on which the saliva is rubbed. The mouth is the first accurate sensory receptor of the body and is often used by children who are still developing the ability to receive and accurately process tactile input through the hand. Always include hand activities to increase accuracy in receiving and processing tactile input as part of an oral program designed to increase sensory-seeking behaviours of the mouth (see chapter 8).

Try:

Enhance the opportunities throughout the day for oral and tactile experiences through a sensory diet (see chapter 8).

Flapping

Why?

This jarring of the body's joints and muscles provides proprioceptive sensation to the muscles and joints of the wrists, arms, and shoulders. This behaviour may be a sign of sensory overload.

Try:

Enhance the opportunities for proprioceptive experiences throughout the day in the sensory diet.

Use the Wilbarger Protocol to reduce sensory defensiveness. Try wall push-ups, jumps with hands held, climbing, and wheelbarrow walks (also, hand-walking with the child's tummy on a physio ball). Have the child play with a Tangle Toy.

Perseverative Play

Why?

Often children with poor body awareness and coordination have poor motor planning. Repetitive play only builds on existing skills and does not require sophisticated motor planning. Every time play changes, the child must plan for the change. The child must actively participate in the environment to plan movement and play. This can be stressful and difficult for children, and they may remain "stuck" in specific movements. The play may feed a visual need for pattern and order (such as lining up cars).

Try:

Build the child's gross and fine motor skills (see chapter 8); provide opportunities to play with toys that require patterning (e.g., puzzles, dominoes, lotto beading, tangrams) because the child may find patterns soothing.

Smelling Behaviours

Why?

The child likely has a low sensitivity to smell and seeks out very strong smells. Remember that the sense of smell is functioning at birth and may be an accurate source of information for the child. Children who enjoy smelling cannot respect personal space because they need to get very close to the other person in order to smell him or her.

Try:

Provide other smelly experiences as part of the sensory diet (e.g., lotion rubs). Offer a "smelling box" with small bottles of different scents. If the child has a fascination for cleaning products, encourage a daily, supervised cleaning chore. Take one or two of the cleaning bottles, rinse, and fill with coloured water, adding a strong smell that he or she enjoys.

Masturbation

Why?

This provides strong tactile stimulation that the child can tolerate. Many children who may have difficulty processing touch have an easier time processing touch from the genitals because the feedback is so strong. Feedback is also predictable. Motor action can be learned quickly and repeated with success. A simple motor action can create strong sensory input. Masturbation is a rhythmic activity, and rhythmic movements are calming.

Try:

Enrich access to calming tactile experiences throughout the day through a sensory diet. Provide opportunities to process sensory input from another part of the body accurately. Add deep pressure, calming input through "weighted" clothes, or pretend to be mummies by wrapping yourselves up tightly with tensor bandages. Roll therapy balls or bolsters over the child (often with your own weight on them) or have the child crawl deep down into a bin filled with plastic balls. Investigate alternative seating for girls, avoiding having them sit on the floor with legs crossed, and for boys, having them sit close to a table where the tabletop prevents access. Use the Wilbarger Protocol to reduce sensory defensiveness.

Pica (mouthing or eating non-food substances, such as dirt and rocks)

Why?

This eating of non-edibles usually provides strong tactile and proprioceptive input for a child who may not be registering sensation. It also may transmit vibration to the jaw, which can stimulate the vibration-sensitive vestibular system.

Try:

Provide a rich vestibular and proprioceptive sensory diet. Use the Wilbarger oral protocol to provide jaw pressure. Find vibrating toys for the child to mouth. Provide something crunchy for oral stimulation at regular times throughout the day.

Sensory-Avoidant Behaviours

Children who avoid certain sensations may be sensory-defensive and trying to protect their nervous systems from sensory overload. There are many avoidant responses, but we will discuss only the most commonly seen behaviours that respond very well to a sensory integration approach. These include

Takes Off Clothing

Why?

This is a clue that the clothes are causing uncomfortable touch input to the skin.

Try:

Use the Wilbarger Protocol to reduce sensory defensiveness. Establish a sensory diet to provide opportunities for calming experiences throughout the day. Look for soft clothing, buy used clothes, or make sure they are well washed prior to wearing.

Avoids Eye Contact

Why?

There are many reasons why children avoid eye contact. Consider these sensory reasons. Peripheral vision may be less stressful than looking directly at something. Processing visual and auditory input may be difficult to do at the same time, so the child looks away in order to process the auditory input more accurately. The child may seek out lines or shapes because looking peripherally changes the visual information.

Try:

Reduce overall sensory defensiveness by enhancing the opportunities for calming experiences throughout the day in the sensory diet and use the Wilbarger Protocol. Build trusting relationships with those around the child. Desensitize with various techniques: teach the child to look in the mirror, look at his own image, and gradually move to looking at people's eyes. By building on the child's strengths and interests (visual patterning and fascination with shapes), point out how people's eyes, together with their noses, form a triangle (if one joined them with lines). If he sees that the mouth is an oval, and that the face itself is an oval he will be more comfortable with eye contact. For the child who does not use direct visual contact, teach body positions that indicate listening (for example, when someone is talking, your hands need to be still).

Avoids Car Rides, Swings, or Any Imposed Movement

Why?

The avoidance of imposed movement suggests this sensation is very frightening to the child.

Try:

Reduce overall sensory defensiveness by enhancing the opportunities for calming experiences throughout the day in the sensory diet. A very gradual introduction to non-threatening vestibular activities should be a long-term goal. Provide proprioceptive sensations during movement to help decrease fear and anxiety (see chapter 8). Encourage parents to drive out of their driveways forward so children can use vision to warn them of movement (backward movement can be frightening). Warn children riding in the car of upcoming turns and stops. Build a safe, padded car seat that offers lots of pressure.

Avoids Stairs or Walking on Different Surfaces

Why?

Some children may experience gravitational insecurity. They are very sensitive to heights and to the demands of gravity. Balance and postural reactions may be immature.

Try:

As in the previous example, a gradual introduction to non-threatening vestibular activities is ideal.

Avoids Handling Sensory Material

Why?

This is a very common sign of tactile defensiveness, as the hands are particularly rich in touch receptors. Often the temperature and wetness of the material make a difference in how well it is tolerated.

Try:

Reduce overall sensory defensiveness by using the Wilbarger Protocol. Provide opportunities for calming tactile and other experiences throughout the day in the sensory diet. Use deep-pressure touch when demonstrating any tactile play (see chapter 8 for tactile activities). Massaging the hands prior to the touch may also be helpful.

Limited Use of Hands for Grasping

Why?

This is another very common sign of tactile defensiveness. Also, as Hanschu and Reisman (1992) state, "The hand without a motor plan is a hand without a purpose." A hand that is not grasping, especially when not tactile defensive, suggests very poor proprioceptive functioning.

Try:

Reduce overall sensory defensiveness by enhancing the opportunities for calming experiences throughout the day as part of the sensory diet. Use the Wilbarger Protocol. Build in many proprioceptive experiences. Use hands in function: opening doors, climbing, grasping the ropes on a swing, etc.

Auditory Sensitivity

Why?

The sensitivity to sounds can differ from sensitivity to speech. Hearing problems and ear infections should be ruled out.

Try:

Reduce overall sensory defensiveness by a sensory diet and use of the Wilbarger Protocol. Help the child gain control over his environment. For example, can the child give clues or verbalize when he feels over-stimulated? Can he tolerate earplugs or use a Walkman? Reassure the child regarding the source of the sound. Chewing gum or other strong proprioceptive jaw input can compete with external noises and calm the nervous system. Fidget toys also may help for the same reason. Teach relaxation techniques (see chapter 5). Consider auditory integration training. Parents, be prepared with an "out-of-order" sign ready to place on hand-dryers in public washrooms to avoid the loud sounds while your child is in that room.

5. A Relaxation Technique for Children

Relaxation training can help everyone deal with stress and anxiety. Children with PDD generally operate under high levels of stress. Current investigations by Groden (1998) indicate that new situations, changes at home or school, seasonal changes, and strong emotional feelings (even extreme excitement, happiness, worry, or anger) can all cause anxiety and stress.

Simple line drawings can effectively teach relaxation techniques (Doan, 1994). To teach children with PDD, these techniques usually need adapting. A traditional relaxation technique that uses auditory, visual, and motor imitation may not be successful if the child has poor body awareness and impaired motor planning.

Adapt sensory integration techniques for a traditional progressive relaxation program. You can easily add tactile and proprioceptive cues or props to the program to enhance success by increasing sensory feedback. Props, such as a squeeze ball, can assist children with motor planning problems because they can provide a clear destination for the desired movement (e.g., squeeze the ball with knees).

Whistles or other blowing toys are often helpful when the child is first learning to take a deep breath on demand. Other children respond to a verbal cue such as "Hold your breath," learned during swimming lessons. Children as young as four have learned this technique and use it well within the classroom setting at routine times or when prompted. Older children need to learn to monitor their own levels of stress and initiate the relaxation technique when required.

Progressive relaxation is a sequenced task. As sequencing is a common weakness in children with motor planning problems, a "book" or card format helps students follow the directions. The child learns to follow the pictured instructions and then turns the page for the next instruction. In order to be successful in reducing stress, relaxation techniques must be learned and then practiced on a regular basis in a variety of settings.

Instructions

The following four pages contain six pictures to cut and fit into a small photo album (4" x 6"). Customize the program by changing the instructions as needed and deciding on a reward or motivator to include on page six. These have been adapted from Doan (1994).

- Prepare a picture or write down the reward, especially for initial learning. Most times a sensory toy or small treat to eat or drink is fine. Extra time to run, jump, or swing may be enough!

- Teach the child to follow the directions on the first page by reading out loud and demonstrating, "Hold the ball and squeeze tight." Skip to the reward page!

- Gradually add pages to the sequence until the child can read the whole "story" and do the required actions, step-by-step, with help. Then gradually do away with the "prompts," the squeeze ball, your hand, or blowing toys.

- Identify what anxiety or over-arousal looks like for the child ("Do I lift my shoulders, chew my lip, cry, feel my heart rate go fast, or start to make noises?").

- Teach children to recognize the emotions they are feeling (e.g., frustration). Teach children to label emotions with words or pictures.

- Help children connect the relaxation techniques that they have used to help calm their feelings. The relaxation techniques found in this book can be made into picture cards to be used within a child's picture communication system.

1. Hold the ball and squeeze tightly.

Now let go; relax.

My Relaxation Book

[Place child's picture here]

Name: _____

3. Squeeze the ball with your shoulders.

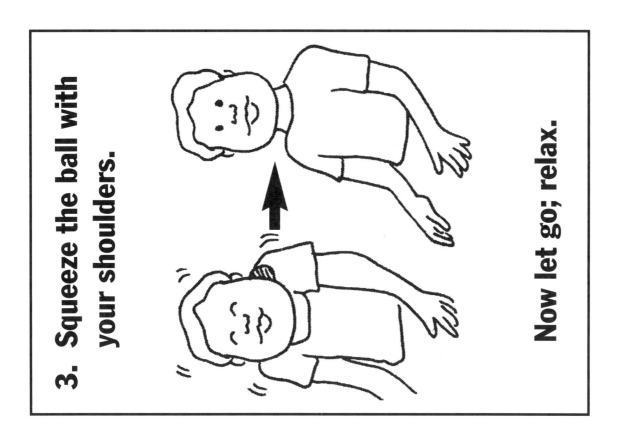

Now let go; relax.

2. Make a "monster" face.

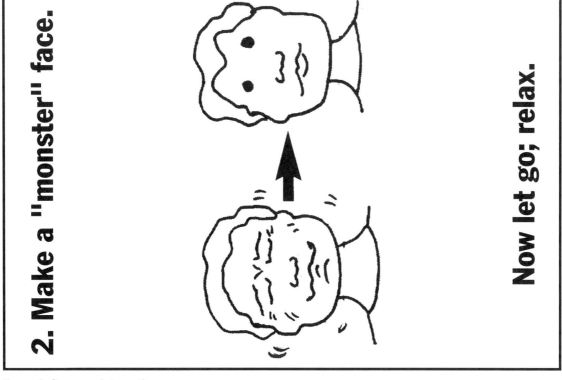

Now let go; relax.

5. Now hold your breath.

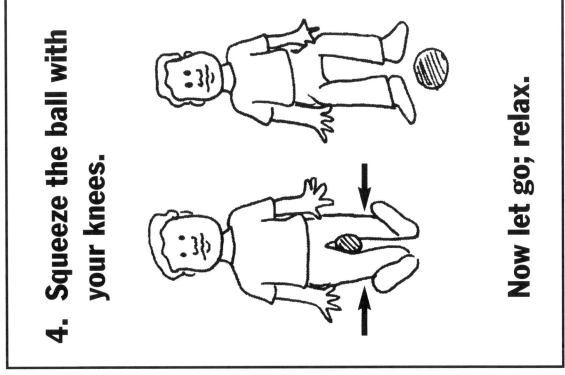

Blow out and relax...

4. Squeeze the ball with your knees.

Now let go; relax.

I did a good job _____

6. Now you are nice and relaxed.

Chapter 6

Ideas for Self-Care Skills

The world can be a very unpredictable place for children with PDD. The sensory information these children receive from their bodies (and from the environment) during self-care skills may be processed incorrectly. Performing self-care activities requires handling of towels, brushes, toothbrushes, and soap. Your child must motor-plan the action and sequence the steps correctly; for example, shampoo must be applied to the hair prior to rinsing. Any other order of this task will not work. To ensure success, your child must pay attention to the task and must monitor the task as he or she is going through it.

> *Alexia hates when her mother towel dries her hair. She winces in pain as the towel absorbs the water. This is an example of a hypersensitive response to sensory input, interpreting the input as painful and alerting.*

Children may also be hypo-responsive to sensory input. They may seek more input in the environment, or they may be oblivious to the sensory input.

> *Ryan does not seem to hear his father calling him to dinner. His father must tap him on the shoulder to get his attention and then tell him it's time for dinner.*

To make matters even more challenging, some children have a fluctuating response to sensory input. Sometimes they are very sensitive to sensory input, and other times they appear to be unaware of sensory input. Remember, factors such as stress, fatigue, and motivation can affect sensory processing.

Children with PDD cannot always respond to the environment, so we must create environments for them that are predictable and feel safe. The predictable environment and approach help alleviate anxiety and maximize neurological processing, interaction, and learning. Routine and consistency are keys to building a learning environment for children where they feel safe and motivated to take the necessary risks for learning.

Remember, working within your child's tolerance allows for the development of trust. Trust can decrease emotional distress. If the environment and those in the environment demonstrate flexibility to the child's needs, your child can relax, let down his guard, and start learning! Good luck with these strategies. We hope you find them helpful.

Sleep

A good night's sleep makes a world of difference to everyone. With a poor sleep pattern, children may not get enough sleep, may not get enough deep sleep, and may have difficulty waking in the morning. Promoting good sleep patterns is a wonderful investment for your child and for you. Remember that pressure touch and neutral warmth are calming to the nervous system.

Sensory Strategies

- ❏ Massage and/or joint compression prior to bed (you can use powder or lotion)
- ❏ Weighted blankets (horse blankets, blankets with weight sewn into them)
- ❏ Wearing wrist/ankle weights to bed
- ❏ Body pillows, sleeping bags
- ❏ Swaddling an infant
- ❏ Different types of pajamas; try tight and loose to determine which type your child prefers (silky or fleece)
- ❏ Avoiding pajamas that have lace or built-in feet (may cause irritation to the child with tactile defensiveness)
- ❏ Checking seams for threads and cover elastic
- ❏ Percale sheets with 240 threads per inch to ensure a smooth bedsheet
- ❏ Bed tent to block out distractions, light, and noise
- ❏ A small night light with a warm glow (but not bright enough to cast shadows) if your child is afraid of the dark
- ❏ Neutral color on the walls
- ❏ Dark blinds to cut down the light
- ❏ Back rubs, bear hugs, and a rub down with a towel with predictable movements
- ❏ Reading in a quiet voice
- ❏ Making a small space for the child to squeeze into—some children like to sleep between the mattress and the box spring, or children may like their bed pushed against the wall so that they can push their bodies against the wall
- ❏ Placing the mattress on the floor if your child is afraid of heights

Other Strategies

- ❏ Predictable routine prior to bed (e.g., bath, teeth, story, bed)
- ❏ Organized room: clean and uncluttered
- ❏ Eliminating rough and tumble play prior to bed, as this may be overstimulating
- ❏ Going to the washroom before bed

Dressing

Dressing involves many skills: visual perception, motor planning, balance, and gross and fine motor skills. Independence in dressing contributes to a real feeling of mastery, which contributes to a healthy self-esteem.

Sensory Strategies

- ❏ Be conscious of sensitivities regarding texture; buy clothing that you know your child will like (it is more valuable for your child to be at school in an uncoordinated outfit feeling calm than to have your child at school looking beautiful and upset)

- ❏ Build a wardrobe of comfortable clothing for your child

- ❏ Encourage deep-pressure activities prior to dressing to decrease the tactile sensitivities

- ❏ Wear undergarments inside out to prevent scratching seams and tags

- ❏ Increase hat tolerance through massage of the scalp and putting the hat on in front of the mirror

- ❏ If your child has difficulty guiding movement with the eyes, encourage another sensory system to compensate (touch)

- ❏ Be aware of audio and visual overload and minimize it

- ❏ Dress the child in front of a mirror to add visual cues to assist with motor planning

- ❏ Break the dressing skill down and have your child do the last activity, then second last, and third last activity, etc.

- ❏ If your child is having difficulty initiating an action, start the action and have your child complete the action (e.g., pulling up a zipper)

- ❏ If your child is fearful when body position is changed, dress him or her in one position (toddlers can have their diapers changed in a standing position)

- ❏ If your child likes to strip, try the Wilbarger Protocol for sensory defensiveness and massage

- ❏ Use augmentative communication strategies to encourage understanding of the consequences of taking clothing off

- ❏ If your child has sensitive feet, have her wear socks inside out and wash shoes to make them soft prior to wearing them

- ❏ Try laced shoes because they can be more effectively tightened

- ❏ Cut labels out of clothing

- ❏ Wash clothing in unscented detergent

- ❏ Dry clothing with unscented fabric softener

- ❏ Dry clothing in a dryer to decrease stiffness

- ❏ Choose softer fabrics like fleece rather than rigid items like denim

- ❏ Be conscious of noises from buckles and overall straps

- ❏ If your child cannot keep his hands out of his diaper or undergarment, try overalls

- ❏ Be sensitive to the length of sleeve and pant leg your child prefers

- ❏ Be aware of patterns in fabrics and distraction the patterns may cause

- ❏ Ensure that the garment fits well; that it is not cutting into the skin when your child assumes another position

Other Strategies

❏ Organize drawers and closets to help enable a child to choose his own clothing

❏ Transitions for seasons may take time: discuss it, prepare for it, use social stories to explain the change

❏ Choose shoes with Velcro® closures and add Velcro to button backs and hoops to zippers for children with fine motor difficulties

❏ Organize clothing the night before and lay the clothing out on the bed

❏ Encourage your child to put away the clothing so that he knows where it belongs

❏ If balancing is difficult, have your child sit to put on socks and shoes

❏ Colour-code clothing to help your child identify right and left

❏ Put labels in your child's clothing to help identify him if he becomes lost

❏ Sing the steps while dressing

❏ Try dressing dolls or teddy bears to practice opening and closing fasteners

❏ Try backward chaining, which involves having your child complete the last step of the activity, then the last two steps, etc.

Grooming

We spend a large portion of our day brushing our hair and teeth and washing our bodies. Our presentation to others is more inviting if we are clean and well-groomed. Difficulty processing touch, poor balance and body awareness, and difficulty motor planning can have a negative effect on our grooming.

Whenever possible, let your child do the task independently. It contributes to self-esteem, and it is easier for the nervous system to process self-imposed touch than touch by another person. If one person is successful in assisting your child with grooming, pay attention to how she does it, what kind of touch she uses, what she says, how close to the child she stands, etc. Others can imitate that style and grooming can be more successful.

General Strategies for Self-Care Skills

❏ Use visual aids to increase your child's understanding of the task (e.g., picture symbols, schedules, sequence strips)

❏ Use communication supports (e.g., social stories, picture symbols)

❏ Build in consistency and predictability to decrease stress

❏ Have an organized environment; put things back in place so your child will be more independent in finding them

❏ Label drawers and clothing to promote independence in putting things away and finding them again

❏ Use calming strategies that are specific to your child

❏ Remember that pressure touch has a more organizing effect than light touch

❏ Minimize sensory input whenever possible

- ❏ To decrease defensiveness, try the Wilbarger Protocol if your child has an exaggerated or uncomfortable response to sensory input
- ❏ Use routines
- ❏ Use motivators
- ❏ Use rhythm and music
- ❏ Practice motor planning–break down skills into smaller components and teach skills one component at a time

Washing

Sensory Strategies

- ❏ Use unscented soap to decrease sensitivities
- ❏ Use a heavy face cloth and use pressure strokes on the body
- ❏ If your child is fearful in balance-related activities, try showering rather than bathing (because there are fewer changes in body position)
- ❏ Water that is warm to the touch is the best temperature; have your child test to ensure comfort
- ❏ Children who are uncomfortable changing the position of their head may not lie down to rinse their hair in the bathtub; try a handheld shower or cover their eyes with a face cloth and use a jug of water to rinse their hair
- ❏ Try to incorporate fascination with water falling from the tap and bubbles into play while washing
- ❏ Dim the lights and minimize sound if your child is easily overwhelmed
- ❏ Be careful that your child doesn't eat the soap
- ❏ Allow choice of shower or bath
- ❏ Try a bathtub rail because children may be frightened getting into and out of the tub (available at your local drugstore)
- ❏ When shampooing, use pressure touch
- ❏ Use pressure and downward strokes with a washcloth and towel if your child is sensitive to touch
- ❏ Use pressure when drying with a towel
- ❏ Dry in front of a mirror and name the body parts to increase your child's body "map"
- ❏ Use a small hand towel to dry as it is less bulky to manage and allows for more visual direction

Other Strategies

- ❏ Tell your child when you plan to touch him or her with the facecloth or toothbrush
- ❏ Use cognitive preparation strategies; for example, "We will wash your right arm and then your left arm"
- ❏ Use visual aids to assist with the comprehension of the task
- ❏ Provide lots of water play in a sink or bowl with fun toys (e.g., squirt gun, boat, diver, squeeze bottle, bubbles, bubble bath, bath foam soap, soap crayons, roll-on soap)

❑ Build up handles of utensils with pipe insulation to decrease dropping

❑ Use music and motivators

Toilet Training

Toilet training can be a real challenge to children with PDD who have sensory integration difficulties. Successful toileting requires receiving and interpreting the sensory information that signals a full bladder or the need to have a bowel movement. The child must form the motor plan to get to the bathroom and then must conquer the sensory challenges of the bathroom.

Toilet training is one of the tasks of childhood that can reflect stress, and a child can exercise a great deal of control by controlling toileting. Try not to enter a battle of wills on the issue. Things tend to run much smoother without stress and expectation. If you experience set backs with your child, know that this is absolutely normal. Take the pressure off and go back at it after some time has passed. The bowel and bladder are smooth muscles, and the sensory signals they send up to the brain to indicate a full bladder or bowel are like soft whispers in comparison to the messages received by striated muscle (in the arm or the leg).

Sensory Strategies

❑ If your child doesn't seem to be aware that he urinating, let him go naked—he will see when he urinates and connect the sensation with the consequence

❑ If your child wears diapers, draw attention to information from other senses, such as smell and added weight of a wet diaper (cloth diapers give more sensory feedback than disposable diapers)

❑ If your child is sensitive to toilet paper, try diaper wipes or a wet face cloth

❑ If your child cannot tolerate sitting on the toilet, try to make it as safe as possible

• Make the hole smaller with an infant toilet seat

• Put a stool under your child's feet

• Try having your child wear a weighted vest to encourage sitting for a longer period of time

• Try a handrail may for your child to hang on to

• Use distractions like books, songs, music, and pictures on the walls

• Children love the feeling of security when they wear a diaper; if they require this security, allow them to wear a diaper while they are on the toilet

• Try a padded toilet seat because it is softer and warmer

❑ If the visual input is too stimulating, turn off the lights or dim them

❑ If the noise is too much, place sound absorbing towels in the bathroom or try earplugs, music, or running water

❑ With smearing of feces, try a bathroom routine with a caregiver present and start a program of strong smells

❑ Never force; respect the child's tolerance

❑ Diaper changes may be difficult if your child is uncomfortable with movement; try changing your child while he stands

Other Strategies

❑ Use visual aids and social stories to increase your child's understanding of the task

❑ Try to make this task as pleasant as possible

Teeth Brushing

Sensory Strategies

❑ If your child is very sensitive, consider using a face cloth to wipe the teeth

❑ If your child is sensitive to touch inside the mouth, try the Wilbarger Protocol for sensory defensiveness (oral program)

❑ To decrease sensitivity, apply pressure to the teeth and gums

❑ Try a Nuk® brush initially, then move to bristles

❑ Use a very mild-flavored toothpaste

❑ Use pressure touch

❑ Promote balance by standing behind your child to secure his body

❑ Try an electric toothbrush—the vibration may be calming

❑ Try joint compression to the head, neck, and shoulders in preparation for teeth brushing

Other Strategies

❑ Encourage frequent water-drinking to remove extra food

❑ Try a footstool to help your child reach the faucets

❑ Facilitate independence in children with fine motor difficulties by using toothpaste in a pump dispenser

Hair Brushing

Sensory Strategies

❑ If your child is sensitive to touch, use a brush with a large head

❑ When brushing, use firm strokes

❑ Brush in front of the mirror so that your child can predict when the brush is coming

❑ Have your child brush her own hair

❑ Use massage to the scalp prior to hair brushing

Other Strategies

❑ Use a conditioner to detangle as much as possible

❑ With tangles, start at the bottom of the hair, holding just above the tangle and then work up to the root

❑ Cut hair short

Hair Cutting

Sensory Strategies

- ❑ Use a mirror and verbal warnings to predict touch
- ❑ Try earphones to block out the noise of the clippers
- ❑ Place downward pressure on the head, through the neck and shoulders
- ❑ Use firm strokes with the comb
- ❑ Blow away all bits of hairs prior to getting dressed
- ❑ Look for a flexible and sensitive hair stylist—it will be worth it
- ❑ Try the Wilbarger Protocol to decrease sensitivities

Other Strategies

- ❑ Use visual aids and social stories to increase understanding of the task
- ❑ Use distraction and motivators
- ❑ Wash your child's hair prior to going to the hairstylist to decrease time spent there
- ❑ Follow up with an enjoyable activity or treat

Eating

No skill creates more anxiety in a parent than eating or lack of eating. Children who have difficulty with this skill may have a heightened sensitivity to touch, smell, or taste. Children who are hypo-sensitive to sensory input may have little awareness of their mouth and how to move their tongue and jaw. They may have a poorly organized suck, swallow, and breath synchrony. Some children have such a need for movement that they may not sit still long enough to eat a meal. Their mealtimes may consist of a mouthful every "lap" around the house.

Other children may be at the other extreme. They use the mouth to discover their world. Edible and non-edible items are mouthed, chewed, and sometimes swallowed. Developmentally, the mouth is the first area of the body that can interpret sensory feedback accurately. As the hands develop in their ability to accurately interpret sensory input, they take over as the primary "investigators" of the environment.

Sensory Strategies

- ❑ Be aware of texture, mix of textures, and temperature of food
- ❑ Encourage the child to "clean" out his mouth with water between mouthfuls of food
- ❑ If your child is orally sensitive, try the Wilbarger Protocol for sensory defensiveness (oral program) or implement an oral desensitization program
- ❑ Apply pressure through the teeth, gums, cheeks, and lips to prepare for food
- ❑ Prepare for eating by massaging with a Nuk gum-massage toothbrush
- ❑ Prepare for eating with movement (e.g., sitting on a bouncing ball, parent's lap, rocker board, etc.)

❏ Use a small make-up mirror at the table to facilitate accuracy in placing the food in the mouth and clean-up after each bite (the visual system can compensate for decreased feedback through the tactile system)

❏ If your child is a messy eater, provide pressure touch around the lips and mouth prior to eating and encourage oral motor activity (e.g., whistling, blowing bubbles) to promote better sensory feedback and build muscle tone for better mouth closure

❏ If your child has difficulty using utensils, try weighted handles, which give more sensory feedback and therefore make movements more accurate

❏ Try a weighted cup, or a cup with a lid and a straw, if your child often spills the drink

❏ Use movement breaks for the active child

❏ Try a gel seat or Move 'n Sit cushion (see Resources) to promote a small amount of movement during sitting

❏ Try a weighted vest to provide the extra input necessary to sit still

❏ If your child is tactile defensive, arrange seating at the end of the table to minimize touch by others

❏ Set up a small "café" table at school or daycare to minimize extra touch

❏ Encourage lots of oral motor play with whistles, harmonicas, kazoos, etc.

❏ Try using ice pops or ice cubes/juice cubes to desensitize the mouth

❏ Minimize overwhelming auditory and visual input

Other Strategies

❏ If your child is slumping in the chair, try some pressure through the shoulders to create the muscle tone to facilitate an upright posture

❏ Work within your child's tolerance

❏ Investigate food allergies, as well as fatigue and appetite

❏ Try different sitting arrangements to facilitate an upright posture and focus

❏ Begin within your child's favorite foods and then increase choices

❏ Model with families and encourage them to model for their child

❏ Encourage your child to request the food that he wants (or "seconds") independently

❏ Try Dycem®, or a similar non-slip material, under your child's plate to keep it in one place

❏ Pre-cut food to encourage independence

❏ Modify utensils to compensate for fine motor and bilateral difficulties

❏ Modify seating to compensate for developing balance

Play

Play is often referred to as the occupation of childhood. Play offers your child the opportunity to develop gross motor, fine motor, visual motor, cognitive, language, imagination, attention, and social skills. Children with PDD often have difficulty with play; therefore, they may be at a disadvantage for learning the necessary skills of childhood.

Play activities are the first social experiences for a child. Play begins as a solitary activity and then becomes parallel (the children are in the same room but do not play together). Finally, play progresses to cooperative play, where children play together—sharing fun, imagination, and skills. Sensory integration difficulties may play a role in why children with PDD may have difficulty with play: problems manipulating toys, poor stamina, and problems with motor planning (creating and sequencing the steps of play in the right order).

Sensory Strategies

❑ If your child has a comfort toy, one that is taken everywhere, wash it frequently and keep it as long as possible (if your child really likes a blanket or toy, try to buy two or three for "insurance")

❑ Children who constantly mouth items can be using their mouths to gather information about their toys, or they may be self-calming—try the Wilbarger Protocol for sensory defensiveness (oral program) and a sensory program in the palms of the hands so that the child can switch from the mouth to the hands

❑ If your child is using mouthing to self-calm, try oral motor activities like chewing, whistles, and bubble blowing, which all provide calming input

❑ Use massage in the palms of the hands; also try weighted wrist cuffs to increase feedback

❑ Some children use touch excessively and may be socially inappropriate in their touching; try teaching limits through social stories

❑ Encourage the child to gather information through vision and use memory to create the information needed

❑ Children with sensitivity to touch may not participate in messy play—try inhibitory techniques: pressure touch, massage, or the Wilbarger Protocol for sensory defensiveness

❑ Encourage your child to participate in messy play using a tool or wearing gloves

❑ Consider temperature and texture of the play material

❑ Grade activities from neat to messy

❑ Use a favorite character or game and integrate a tactile component into it; use motivation to get over the hurdle of avoidance

❑ Children who are sensitive to balance activities may not participate in playground games or games where their feet are off the ground—try massage, joint compression, and "heavy work" activities prior to going on the equipment

❑ Respect your child's fear

❑ Use routines that can be calming because they are so predictable

❑ If your child seems to be unaware of playground boundaries, try using a homemade stop sign along with proprioceptive input

❑ Encourage your child to slow down and learn about body position and balance by creating an obstacle course on the playground equipment

❑ If your child is uncomfortable in any positions, inform his caregiver and teacher to avoid stressful situations

❑ If your child is afraid of swings, address the underlying skills of strength, balance, coordination, etc.

- ❏ If your child always breaks toys and the tips of pencils, teach the difference between light and heavy touch, and practice playing with specific toys while working on the underlying areas of development

- ❏ If your child is impulsive in play, break down the task into small steps

- ❏ Teach each step in the style your child learns best—auditory, visual through demonstration, or by guiding the child through the movement (please see motor planning section for more strategies)

- ❏ Cause and effect toys are excellent for children with motor planning difficulties

- ❏ Give children a feeling of control and anticipation with predictable toys

- ❏ Always look at function—what toy will enable your child to use the behaviour functionally?

- ❏ If your child chews on toys, provide a "chewie" (e.g., gum, chewy candy, pacifier, etc.) to increase oral motor input so that your child can play

- ❏ If your child needs movement to stay organized, try playing on a swing or moving surface

- ❏ Watch your child's eyes; if visual tracking is difficult, place toys within the central visual field

- ❏ Be aware of light intensity; your child may need to wear sunglasses

- ❏ Encourage play with sounds within your child's tolerance

- ❏ Minimize background noise since it may be hard for your child to discriminate between sounds

- ❏ Be aware of smell; wash toys with an unscented soap

Other Strategies

- ❏ Attach language to each step

- ❏ Try taking turns during play and teaching your child to pause and "check-in" with their friends

- ❏ Give lots of opportunities for gross motor play and alternate between gross and fine motor play

- ❏ Make play motivating and fun

- ❏ Teach play skills

- ❏ Encourage a willingness to share and communication of affection and appreciation for the efforts of others

- ❏ Modify toys for fine motor difficulty

Chapter 7

Adapting Home, School, and Childcare Settings

All children function better in a predictable environment. This can be as simple as having a tidy room and storage for their own things. Providing routine and structure can compensate for your child's difficulty with language, sequencing, attention shift, and memory. Developing habits or consistent ways of doing things is very helpful and can reduce stress for most children with PDD. It also provides more consistent and reliable sensory information. As the child grasps the new learning, this learning can be generalized across settings and between caregivers. Introduction of small changes to the task, as the child can tolerate, can contribute to better problem solving abilities and the ability to generalize the skill. Generalization promotes flexibility in the skill that makes the skill functional and useable.

> *Susie knows she always eats in the kitchen. She knows that her shoes, jacket, and backpack are always at the side door, and she knows she sleeps in her own bed. This consistency in her environment reduces Susie's behavioural outbursts.*

If we have a consistent place for our car keys, we know where to find them each time we use the car. Many of us spend stressful moments looking for the car keys while waving goodbye to any chance of punctuality.

We need to consider consistency in the environment, schedule, and approach with children with autism/PDD. If we study the child's individual style, we can strive for consistency across environments—at home, at grandma's, in the classroom, and in the childcare setting.

Children spend most of their time at home. It is the first environment they know. Their favorite people live there, so home can be a place of relaxation and a place of learning. Many families use the home as the first school for children. Activities that offer your child the opportunity to integrate sensory information can be incorporated right into your home. Take into account your space, the needs of other family members, and the needs of your child prior to purchasing equipment. A consistent play area and an organized home will offer your child the chance to regulate activity level and increase his or her comfort and relaxation. Organization can give children with PDD a sense of control because they are able to predict their day.

Transition times, the times between activities or environments, are often stressful for children with PDD. There is a whole new set of expectations that demand attention, processing, and motor planning. Change is almost always difficult, and there should be a sensory plan in place with a visual schedule. The room should be set up so there is an opportunity for children to do a familiar "safe" activity right away. Other children may participate in the sensory plan. Sensory strategies are listed to give the reader ideas to compensate for sensory integrative dysfunction and make use of the sensory systems the child can process best. We have also included some general strategies to provide ideas that do not have a sensory base, but we have found them helpful in our work with children with PDD.

Environmental Accommodations—Home

Sensory Strategies For the Home

- ❏ In your home, offer "hide-out" places like beanbag chairs, small tents, pillow corners
- ❏ Use soft objects, rugs, and pillows to absorb noise
- ❏ Decrease visual stimuli and auditory stimuli to decrease distraction
- ❏ Use body pillows, weighted blankets, heavy quilts, or weighted vests to offer calming input
- ❏ Have the right type and amount of light for your child
- ❏ Use timers to alert your child to the beginning and end of an activity
- ❏ Try to schedule calming activities in between more-demanding activities to maintain a calm nervous system (see sensory diet section)
- ❏ Pay attention to the type of person to which your child responds well (voice, volume, proximity, style, verbal and facial expression)
- ❏ Have "heavy jobs" available for your child (eg., carrying in groceries, carrying laundry, dragging the clothesline in and pushing it out, watering flowers with a heavy watering can, pushing the grocery cart, stacking cans in the food cupboard)
- ❏ If your child responds well to movement, have a quiet place in your home to hang a hammock swing or porch swing
- ❏ A water bed, which is soft and warm, can be comforting and relaxing
- ❏ Be conscious of your child's response to colour
- ❏ Use dark blinds to minimize strong sunlight, streetlights, and cars at night
- ❏ Use soft lights reflected against a wall to decrease visual glare
- ❏ Paint your child's room a soft pastel colour and do not fill the walls with visual distraction
- ❏ If your child needs lots of visual stimulation, consider painting his or her room a bright colour and adding mobiles
- ❏ Provide a sleeping bag for your child to curl up in
- ❏ Children with sensitive hearing should have their bedrooms in a quiet corner of the house
- ❏ Be aware of background noise from the radio, television, and telephone

General Strategies for the Home

- ❏ Minimize clutter; put extra toys and clothes in boxes and label them
- ❏ Have a specific place for objects so that your child (and you!) can find them easily, and encourage your child to return items where they belong
- ❏ Use visual aids to assist in the understanding of tasks
- ❏ Use a schedule to let your child know what will be happening that morning
- ❏ Break chores down into small steps to facilitate learning; give your child enough time to process the directions
- ❏ Use a timer to help your child complete tasks
- ❏ Establish routines and be consistent in following them; this helps your child predict upcoming events and feel calm

- ❏ Prepare for school (clothing, lunch, and homework) the evening before to minimize stress the next morning
- ❏ Prepare your child for changes by using visual and communication aids
- ❏ Use touch to get your child's attention if calling his or her name does not work
- ❏ Whenever possible, give visual cues when giving directions
- ❏ Enjoy each other's company!

Other Home Strategies

Many children will benefit from having the environment set up to provide calming input such as music, pressure touch with lotion, slow rhythmic swinging in straight planes of movement, slow rocking, sitting on a therapy ball, or an oral activity like drinking with a straw from their own water bottle. Children may be participating in the Wilbarger Protocol for sensory defensiveness or may have an organized sensory diet that has been set up by an occupational therapist.

Auditory and visual preparation ahead of time can assist in transitions. Timers, clocks with alarms, watches (with a timer), and concrete transitional objects may be helpful during transitions. Children can benefit from use of a concrete transitional object because they can associate that object with the transitional task. For example, handing Andy her jacket facilitates her ability to get ready for recess. She understands the task and transitions well. Without this understanding, children can resist the change even though a favorite activity is next.

Please refer to chapter 6 for strategies specific to self-care skills.

Playground Equipment for Home and School

In our clinical experience, we have seen the most success with programs or homes that offer access to lots of movement, pressure touch, and consistency. Following is a list of suggested items. An occupational therapist can help guide your choice of equipment.

Suppliers and instructions for "make your own" items are provided in the appendix of this book.

- ❏ Outdoor trampoline
- ❏ Mini-trampoline inside
- ❏ Large therapy or hop balls
- ❏ Swings—inner tube type, platform swing, hammock, sling swing, disc swing
- ❏ Beanbag chairs
- ❏ Small child-sized table and chair
- ❏ Sandbox or sensory bins
- ❏ Tent ball pit, large box with cushions, or homemade "fort" to provide a safe place to retreat
- ❏ Soft surfaces to "crash and bump," like big pillows and old mattresses
- ❏ Weighted objects to play with and throw (e.g., beanbags, beach balls filled with water)
- ❏ Small "fidget" toys for the hand or mouth

- ❑ General messy play and tactile adventures
- ❑ Edible fine motor and oral motor activities
- ❑ Scooterboards
- ❑ Rocker boards
- ❑ Gel seats

This list is by no means complete. Use your imagination and the imagination of your child to add to this list. Dollar stores, second hand stores, and garage sales are great sources for toys and equipment. Always be aware of safety concerns and ensure supervision. An occupational therapist can customize a program for your child's needs. Updates to the program can also be provided on a regular basis to support new learning.

Monitor the wear and tear on your equipment and have fun.

Environmental Accommodations in School and Childcare Settings

Communication between the Home and School

Children with PDD often thrive with consistency and routine. Skills will be learned more quickly and generalized more easily if they can be practiced both at school and at home. This consistency in approach is dependent upon good communication. Many schools and childcare centres have a communication book already set up between home and school. Parents are very dependent upon this book for feedback regarding their child's day, especially if their child's communication skills are developing. The communication sheet outlines important points that should be shared between home and school for the benefit of your child.

Creativity is the most important tool in modifying the school and childcare setting for the child with PDD. We must often step outside our traditional role of teacher, childcare worker, or therapist to accommodate the needs of children with PDD. Use abilities, interests, and even perseverative behaviours to accommodate the areas of difficulty. Remember, we must modify the environment and our approach as the children may not be able to accommodate their behaviours to the school environment.

Each child with PDD has a unique set of abilities and difficulties; consider the individual child, not the label, when creating your program. Incorporation of strategies and modification of the environment can go a long way in promoting independence and function of the child with PDD.

There are many strategies in this section. If you try a strategy and find that it is not helpful, do not give up. Problem-solve with your colleagues and teammates; perhaps you need to try the strategy in a different way, at a different time of the day, or maybe you need to try a new strategy. Some children seem to know when you are trying to understand them, and they will be patient as you "learn the ropes."

"Fixations"—We often view fixations as problems, but like clouds with silver linings, they can be great assets to your program. Fixations can act as motivators, and motivators can increase a sense of calm and increase the ability to focus attention. Scheduling fixations into the routine of the day or using fixations to teach concepts can be very helpful.

> *Ian loved trains. He would line them up over and over again and watch the wheels turn. His teacher painted letters on each train car and taught Ian how to spell small words by arranging the train cars in order. Ian was thrilled because he got to participate in his favorite activity, and his teacher was thrilled that Ian learned the concept so easily.*

Children with PDD may have difficulty processing information from more than one sensory channel at a time. Eye contact may be especially difficult for children with PDD. "Listen to me," rather than "Look at me," may be a more helpful approach. Remember that meaning is most easily attached to visual and tactile input. A functional approach is most effective because it is concrete. Children with PDD may not easily understand abstract skills. For example, practice writing letters on the schedule board where they will be used rather than practicing them in a printing book.

A tape recorder cannot record sound and play sound at the same time. Some children have the same difficulty; it takes them time to process the sensory information received during the school day and switch to the output channel where they can express their knowledge. Good communication between the home and school can accommodate this delay in switching "channels." Use a communication book daily and communicate verbally as often as possible (even by taped messages). The school and childcare settings offer lots of wonderful sensory input; however, this input can be overwhelming to the child with PDD.

School and Childcare Sensory Strategies

- ❑ Remember that visual information is often better organized than verbal information
- ❑ Minimize visual clutter
- ❑ Define physical space—Where is the child's seat? Where is the door? Where are the scissors? (Keep things in a consistent place to increase independence in school tasks).
- ❑ Build sensory activities into the entire day so that the student's nervous system can be maintained in a calm state (sensory diet)
- ❑ Allow for self-soothing behaviours
- ❑ Incorporate self-soothing behaviours into function
- ❑ Investigate the use of weighted vests, hats, and wrist cuffs during the school day
- ❑ Build movement breaks into the child's schedule
- ❑ Be aware of sensory processing; if there is a difficulty, offer input through one sensory channel at a time
- ❑ Time is often needed to switch from taking in information and the ability to express new learning
- ❑ Determine the focus of the activity; is it a sensory need or to develop motor skills?

- ❏ Use a calm, consistent loving tone when speaking with the child
- ❏ Use colour-coded binders to help keep work in order
- ❏ Use the strongest sensory systems to teach new activities
- ❏ Use a physical prompt to start a movement
- ❏ Remove sources of loud, unpredictable noises (e.g., PA system), or warn the child before the PA system goes on
- ❏ Use oral motor strategies to build attention and a sense of calm
- ❏ Give the child frequent movement breaks
- ❏ Provide a quiet corner with a tent or pillows where the child can go and relax and refocus
- ❏ Keep rules of the daycare/school setting consistent
- ❏ Have a rocking chair available for calming
- ❏ Make an "office" out of a large box, which can be a quiet place to do work

General Strategies

- ❏ Use communication aids and visual strategies to enable the child to understand requests and upcoming events of the day
- ❏ Make new learning as concrete as possible
- ❏ Remember that tasks are easier to learn if they make sense to the child
- ❏ Use a plasticized timetable
- ❏ Use sequence boards
- ❏ Use activity checklists
- ❏ Give ample time to prepare for change
- ❏ Use humor; it works wonders for everyone
- ❏ Use timers to signal the end of an activity
- ❏ Learn about successful strategies used at home and use these in school
- ❏ Use motivators to promote attention and focus
- ❏ Give the child some control in the daycare or school setting; allow for choices
- ❏ Keep environment, routine, and verbal directions as consistent as possible
- ❏ Communicate daily between teachers, parents, therapists, and other caregiver— both orally and in writing

Physical Space

Sensory Strategies

- ❏ Place the student in a place where he can see and hear well to facilitate learning
- ❏ If the child is uncomfortable with touch, place the desk away from traffic and, if possible, facing the classroom with his back against a wall
- ❏ If there is a light sensitivity, do not seat the child near the window
- ❏ Encourage a child who is sensitive to light to wear a visor or sunglasses

- ❏ If the child is uncomfortable when her feet are not connected with the earth, have chairs low to the ground where the feet can touch, or place a little stool under her feet
- ❏ If the child often slips out of her seat, try using a non-slip rubber surface on the chair and under the book she's working on
- ❏ If sitting posture is a problem, offer movement breaks, T-stools, large balls, or gel seats to sit on
- ❏ Encourage the child to sit with legs crossed in front, not behind
- ❏ Offer a safe "hide-out" place in the classroom
- ❏ Allow students to do their work where they feel most comfortable
- ❏ When lining up, encourage the child who has difficulty processing touch to stand at the front or the back of the line
- ❏ If the child likes to chew items, have oral motor activities available (e.g., beverage tubing, harmonicas, bubble toys, etc.)

General Strategy

- ❏ Use visual cues on the floor to help guide the child to a specific activity or place

Sitting and Staying in Circle

Sensory Strategies

- ❏ Try a beanbag chair or soft chair that will give support through a large portion of the body's surface
- ❏ Use a carpet square to designate the child's place
- ❏ If necessary, use a chair to sit in while participating in the circle
- ❏ Be aware of tactile feedback from classmates
- ❏ Have special toys that are only used during this time (e.g., fidget toys, vibrating toys, or other favorite toys)
- ❏ Assist with attention by encouraging movement, which provides proprioceptive, kinaesthetic, and vestibular input prior to and during sitting (e.g., move 'n sit, T-stool, large ball)
- ❏ Tickle the child on the back and back of the neck to maintain attention

General Strategies

- ❏ Work within success; if your child can stay in circle well for 20 seconds, use this as your baseline and increase time from this point—try to make it positive
- ❏ Try a short walk around the circle and then try sitting again
- ❏ Try music to draw attention and focus
- ❏ Allow the child to sit beside the teacher and hand over items for discussion to help maintain attention

Physical Education/Exercise Time

Sensory Strategies

- ❏ Use motivating music to attract the child
- ❏ Have a designated area for movement that is safe and open
- ❏ If necessary, offer the child the opportunity to move apart from the other children
- ❏ Be cautious of the auditory feedback of large rooms (like the school gym) because the child may not be able to tolerate the sound
- ❏ Encourage activities that invite creative movement so that the child, no matter how he moves, will be correct (e.g., animal walks, "stop and go," and obstacle courses are good places to start)
- ❏ Encourage heavy proprioceptive dance for organization and enjoyment
- ❏ When learning a specific movement, break the task down and teach in "bite-sized" pieces
- ❏ Increase memory for movements by repeating them several times to music
- ❏ If the child is fearful of heights, try wearing weighted vests, cuffs, hats, etc.
- ❏ Teach steps of a larger sport (e.g., teach the child how to be a goalie in soccer rather than the whole game)
- ❏ Build endurance in children with low muscle tone through a general stamina building program (e.g., swimming, stair climbing, walking)
- ❏ Attach language to movement
- ❏ Use familiar movements and modify them slowly allowing the child time to problem solve
- ❏ Follow the child's lead; leave an activity open from time to time to observe organization of the task

Manipulatives

Sensory Strategies

- ❏ The child may mouth puzzle pieces or other small parts of activities—try offering an appropriate chew toy or a piece of tubing to chew on while playing with the manipulative
- ❏ The child may tap on pieces to increase auditory feedback (or because he or she doesn't know how to play with the toy)—to decrease tapping, teach the child how to play with the toy or try using only one hand
- ❏ Try teaching with a strong sensory base; for example, try putting a shape sorter in the sand table; use the sensory input to maintain attention to the task while learning the task

General Strategies

- ❏ Try hand-over-hand teaching with lots of positive reinforcement
- ❏ Try singing while you are doing the activity ("Here We Go Round the Mulberry Bush" can be adapted to just about anything!)

Sensory Activities

These are often the favorite activities. The child may want to get right into the sensory bin, may mouth the material, may pour it out onto the floor, or may throw it to get the attention of the teacher or other children—try to determine the reason behind the behaviour.

Sensory Strategies

❑ Use massage/pressure touch prior to the activity to give the rest of the body sensory input and decrease the desire to lie in the sensory bin

❑ Provide the child with a chewie or similar oral activity to keep the mouth busy while the hands are learning

❑ Massage the hands prior to sensory play to get children "ready" to receive the input and decrease the use of the mouth

❑ Have a pouring activity in the sensory bin—a revolving wheel, strainers, spoons, bowls, and an incline—especially if the child likes to "watch" items falling down

❑ Place a piece of plastic or a large bowl on the floor to catch the material—this works for the child who likes to pour things onto the floor

❑ Structure the play with a game and take turns to provide the child with attention and a feeling of being a part of play

General Strategies

❑ If the child wants to get his whole body into the activity, use a visual strategy to explain that this is not the way to play

❑ Praise play that is appropriate to the activity and praise often

❑ Model play and guide interaction with other children at the sensory table

❑ Keep the child involved in the activity; sing, take turns pouring

Washroom Time

Sensory Strategies

❑ Waiting for a turn to use the washroom or wash hands may be difficult, so try to have another activity set up for the child to do while waiting (e.g., books, sensory play, songs, or fidget toys)

❑ The toilet may be a challenge due to gravitational insecurity; try using a potty or a potty seat that makes the hole smaller, have the feet firmly "planted" on a foot stool, offer the child your hands to hold, read a book, or sing a favorite song

❑ Children may need to void in a diaper because of the sensory feedback it provides; try wearing the diaper to void while sitting on the toilet (when the child is ready to take the diaper off, it may be useful to cover the hole with white tissue paper to decrease the visually perceived depth of the hole in the toilet)

❑ If the temperature of the toilet seat is uncomfortable, try a cushioned seat or use a towel over the seat with a hole cut out of it

❑ Lying back on a change table may be difficult due to discomfort with lying on the back; try holding the child's head while he is lying down or try changing the child while he is standing up

General Strategies

❑ Respect the child's tolerance and never force an activity—the child might become anxious

❑ Positively reward efforts and attempts

Working within the child's tolerance allows for the development of trust between the teacher and the child. It also avoids the increase in emotional distress that seems to be particularly difficult for these children. If the environment and the teacher respect the child and demonstrate flexibility, the child can relax, let down her guard, and begin to learn. The child can put energy used in being protective and stressed into learning. It is the responsibility of the environment and people in that environment to create the setting for learning.

Snack Time

Sensory Strategies

❑ If the child is uncomfortable with touch, sit at the table end as touch is minimized without neighbours

❑ If the child slumps or rolls out of the chair, try some pressure touch through the shoulders and head

❑ Try posture pillows to support posture

❑ Have the child wear a weighted vest or a wrist weight for poor body awareness

❑ Teach utensil use by initially giving the child food items that can be speared by a fork and then teaching hand over hand

❑ Try plastic or wood utensils (or plasticine over the spoon handle) for the child who is uncomfortable with cold, metal utensils

❑ Children with tactile defensiveness may not be able to tolerate more than one texture in their food; pureé food to ensure consistency of texture

❑ Respect temperature preferences

❑ Introduce foods in similar texture groups

❑ Use thicker textures of food for children with poor mouth-closure and difficulty coordinating tongue movements

❑ Use a non-slip material under the child's plate and cup to prevent movement

❑ Build up handles of utensils with pipe insulation

❑ Try using a mirror to increase visual feedback regarding the face

❑ Teach the child to use the napkin to wipe the face after eating

❑ Use a weighted cup to help with accuracy

❑ Give the child a cup with a lid to decrease mess while the child is learning this skill

❑ Provide movement breaks if necessary

❑ If the child is fearful having her feet off of the floor, ensure she eats at a small table and chair or place a footstool under her feet at a larger table

❑ If the child finds sitting with all the other children overwhelming, set up a small cafe table and encourage the child to invite one other child to eat with him to have snack

General Strategies

❑ If food is a motivator, use it as an excellent learning opportunity because attention and focus will be enhanced

❑ Give a small amount of food at a time to encourage the child to ask for more

- ❏ Encourage independent clean up where the child brings the bowl and cup to the kitchen to be cleaned
- ❏ Ensure correct table and chair heights; build up the height with a booster seat if necessary
- ❏ If anxiety is high, the child may not eat well; ensure a calm, comfortable environment during mealtime

Music

Sensory Strategies

- ❏ Use headphones when necessary with children who have sensitive hearing
- ❏ Be aware of sound preferences
- ❏ Be aware of fluctuating volume
- ❏ Warn the child before an unexpected or loud sound
- ❏ Whenever possible, give the control to the child; let her turn the music on and off
- ❏ Offer consistency in songs to encourage memory and the ability to sing along
- ❏ Be aware of the child with tactile defensiveness and her position to others in the music class
- ❏ Offer fidget toys to increase attention and focus or provide a musical instrument to play

General Strategies

- ❏ Use music often if motivating
- ❏ Use visual strategies to assist with understanding
- ❏ Have a list of activities to increase the child's ability to predict what comes next
- ❏ Music is so motivating; use it to work on
  - Turn taking—using a song like "Old MacDonald"
  - Eye contact—withholding the next verse until the child connects verbally or with eye contact
  - Interaction
  - Incorporation of movement and rhythm
  - Sequencing of activities (due to the predictability of the song)

Fine Motor Work

Sensory Strategies

- ❏ Offer sensory play to the child who is developing fine motor skills
- ❏ Build up the handles of writing utensils with pencil grips and pipe insulation to make them easier to grip
- ❏ Use weight on writing utensils for the child who is developing body awareness
- ❏ If the child is sensitive to feedback through the hand, massage the hand prior to fine motor work
- ❏ If the child cannot accept touch through the hands, have her wear gloves during sensory play
- ❏ Use a glue stick rather than sticky, tacky glue for the child who dislikes textures

- ❑ If the child is developing body awareness, have her wear a wrist weight
- ❑ Have her wear a weighted vest to increase attention and information regarding the position of the body
- ❑ Put weight on the shoulder to increase awareness
- ❑ Provide a physical prompt to get started
- ❑ Try a gel seat or a T-stool for the child who needs movement to increase attention

General Strategies

- ❑ Use visual strategies for sequencing tasks
- ❑ Decrease the amount of written work by considering quality versus quantity of written work
- ❑ Use another method for expression of knowledge: tape recorder, oral response, multiple choice questions, etc.
- ❑ Provide more time for assignments and encourage self-checking
- ❑ Use a computer to write
- ❑ Give math problems that are already written out and have the child only write the answer
- ❑ Use graph paper in math to help keep the numbers in the correct place
- ❑ Have the child circle or underline the correct answer rather than writing it out
- ❑ Break large projects down into small "bites"
- ❑ Have the child write on a vertical surface rather than a horizontal surface (e.g., taping the paper to the blackboard or using an easel)
- ❑ Have a stamp with the child's name to decrease the need to write his name many times
- ❑ Glue correct answers on a prepared sheet rather than writing them
- ❑ Watch for perseverative behaviours
- ❑ Be aware that cognitive functioning may not be on the same level as the writing skill
- ❑ When the child is having difficulty, try to determine if the concept is the challenge or the fine motor work is the challenge
- ❑ Ensure proper table and chair heights where the feet are resting on the floor and the elbows can be comfortably held at a 90-degree angle

Social

Sensory Strategies

- ❑ If proximity to others is hard to handle, encourage the child to be at the front or the back of the line in order to minimize touch by others
- ❑ Be aware of negative reactions to touch as the student may respond to random, light touch with aggression
- ❑ Teach other students to alert the child that they are approaching, especially when they are approaching from behind (this is especially true for students who can become fearful of new sensory input)
- ❑ If the child has tactile defensiveness, encourage interaction games that offer distance (e.g., rolling a ball back and forth)
- ❑ If the child needs pressure touch, teach appropriate ways to get it (e.g., doing wall push-offs rather than hugging his friend all the time)

❑ If the child has developing balance skills, position her where there is something "safe" to grab onto if balance is threatened

❑ Teach other students to use visual cues to initiate interaction with a child who does not seem to hear

❑ Minimize sound if the child is sensitive; talk in whispers; take turns speaking to prevent overstimulation

❑ Teach sensory strategies to peers

❑ Teach children how to respect the personal space of others

❑ Use active games or sensory play to encourage interaction (this may be the first type of activity that will work)

❑ Teach the child to gather information through vision instead of only touch

❑ Provide self-regulatory strategies to enable the child to keep calm and organized

General Strategies

❑ Do not demand eye contact and teach others in the school setting that eye contact can be very stressful to the child

❑ Promote listening by saying, "Listen to me" not "Look at me"

❑ Use social stories to explain rules and social situations

❑ Use augmentative communication strategies (if necessary) and teach fellow students how to use this system so that they can interact

❑ Build opportunities for social interactions by structuring them; have the student hand out the books, hold the door, collect the trip money, etc.

❑ Promote independence in self-care

❑ Provide choices to promote independence and interaction

❑ Model shaking hands and other social skills for the student who may need strategies for displaying and receiving emotion or a

❑ If the child has difficulty finding a friend due to poor visual scanning, teach how to call out his friend's name

❑ Encourage interaction through activities and play rather than by verbal interaction

❑ Practice taking turns—make it fun

❑ Have the child practice cleaning up after herself

❑ Encourage the child to be responsible for a job in order to be a contributing member of the family and class

❑ Practice role playing, plays, skits, and puppet plays to build interaction within the safety of a script

❑ Teach the child how to play board games to provide a structured setting for social interaction

❑ Encourage employment where social interaction is structured (e.g., waiter; "Can I get your order? Would you like French fries as well?")

Preparation for the School Years Ahead...

Greater independence in self-care, along with the ability to organize work and get along with others, will result in more choices in education for the child. Early attention to these areas will pay off in the future. Independence in these areas contributes to a sense of mastery and control over the immediate environment that leads to greater self-esteem and confidence. A feeling of mastery also contributes to more organized behaviour as movements have more purpose and frustration is minimized.

- ❑ Provide school setting support that is appropriate to the child's independence in self-care
- ❑ Make home life easier for parents by establishing predictable routines that help the child with motor planning difficulties to prepare for activities
- ❑ Determine which sensory channels are best perceived by the child and try to teach via these channels
- ❑ Use interests and adapt these interests to learn new skills
- ❑ Use movement and pressure touch to prepare for an activity
- ❑ Practice turn taking and waiting skills to prepare for lining up and for communication
- ❑ Teach how to sit and participate in an activity
- ❑ Help the child understand which activities offer calming and how to identify rising anxiety
- ❑ Help the child connect her rising anxiety with calming strategies
- ❑ Teach the child how to tell others in the environment that the calming strategy is needed
- ❑ Encourage a willingness to share and communicate affection and appreciation (Model respect, affection, and shaping responses)

Problem-Solving Worksheet

For Students with Sensory Integration Dysfunction

Students with sensory integration dysfunction often have behaviour that can disrupt a classroom and interfere with a student's learning. With the following list of questions, a school team can problem solve around the behaviours that a child with PDD may exhibit. Remember that each student is unique, and behaviours can be motivated by different factors. This is detective work, and answers may not be obvious. Careful observations and investigation can really pay off. Encourage the student's participation in order to observe motor planning, sensory processing, and the ability to persevere at a task. Strategies to modify behaviours can enhance your student's learning and participation in the classroom setting.

Child's name: _____

Occupational therapist: _____

Observed behaviours: _____

_____

1. What underlies the behaviour?

- Try to understand the reason behind the behaviour you are observing.
- Let the student know you are attempting to understand and that you know he or she is trying hard to be respectful.
- Have members of your team fill out questionnaires to broaden your information base.
- Observe the student and observe responses to different sensory stimuli at different times of the day (take into account fatigue, transitions, etc.)

When do atypical behaviors occur? _____

_____

What helps the student stop atypical behaviours? _____

_____

2. What motivates this student?

Are there sensory motivators that this student uses to self-calm? _____

_____

Are there toys, activities, topics, or music that motivate this student? _____

_____

_____

3. Can the behaviour be altered so that

It is acceptable in the classroom setting? _____

_____

The student's need is being met? _____

_____

Over

4. Can the schedule and/or the environment be changed to accommodate the student's needs?

Can activities requiring more organization and concentration be scheduled at the beginning of the day?

_____

_____

Can there be quiet times so that the teacher is available for more individual attention?_____

_____

_____

Can offensive sensory stimuli be minimized and organizing sensory stimuli be increased? _____

_____

_____

Can calming sensory stimuli be scheduled into the child's day to increase calmness (sensory diet)? _____

_____

_____

5. Does structure and routine facilitate the student's ability to predict upcoming events?

Can communication aids become part of the student's organization to increase understanding of the day's events and to give a sense of control? _____

_____

_____

6. Can the perception of sensory stimuli be changed?

Can wearing weighted vests, ear plugs, or Irlen lenses be introduced? _____

_____

_____

Can verbal or visual strategies be incorporated? How? _____

_____

_____

7. How can communication among members of the school team, home, and community agencies be facilitated to ensure consistent strategies and understanding across environments?

_____

_____

8. Other Strategies

_____

_____

_____

_____

_____

_____

_____

Communication between Home and School

Children with PDD often thrive with consistency and routine. Skills will be learned more quickly and generalized more easily if they can be practiced both at home and school. This consistency in approach is dependant upon good communication. Many schools and childcare centres have a book of communication sheets already set up between home and school.

Parents need this book for feedback regarding their child's day, especially if their child's communications skills are developing. The communication sheet should outline important points that should be shared between home and school for the benefit of the child. The sample communication sheet on the following page lists activities on each line and includes columns for noting information about each activitity.

Activity

This section asks you to name the activity in which the child participated.

Goals of the Activity

What is the purpose behind doing this activity? Some suggestions include socialization, learning independence in the tasks of daily life, cognitive skills, fine motor skills, gross motor skills, language, communication, music, taking turns, etc.

Child's Performance

How did the child do at this activity? Be specific so that performance can be measured later on in the school year (against the present time). How independent was the child? Did he enjoy the activity? How long did he stay at the activity?

Strategies

Was the activity modified? How? Was the environment modified? How? Were any visual strategies used? Which ones were used, and how were they used? Any auditory strategies? Which ones and how were they used? Any strategies to compensate for motor planning difficulties? Which ones and how were they used?

Home/School Ideas

Ideas for Home: What activities could be practiced at home to strengthen this child's understanding and independence in this task?

Ideas for School: What activities could be reviewed at school to support new learning done at home?

Chart on reverse

Communication Between Home and School

Activity	Goals of Activity	Child's Performance	Strategies Used	Home Ideas

Keeping Calm in the Classroom

We need to provide an environment for learning that puts the child with sensory integration difficulties in a calm, ready state. If the child appearsanxious, there are several interventions that have proved successful (Groden, 1994). There are many other strategies that by "trial and error" have been observed to significantly lower anxiety (learning is not taking place if anxious behaviours occurs).

Anxiety presents in many forms and may look like gaze aversion, hand flapping, biting, increased tactile defensiveness (negative reaction to touch), or other irregular motor behaviours. Calming techniques and/or removing oneself from the sensory-overloading situation are often needed.

Fidget Baskets—look for small, quiet toys—items that will not disturb the other children

- Silly putty® (see chapter 9 for a recipe to make your own)
- Stress balls (Theraband® makes a wonderful red ball and discount stores often have soft squishy balls or toy animals)
- Flour balloon (see chapter 9 for a recipe to make your own)
- Fidget Bag Toys (see chapter 9 for more ideas)

Things to Wear—to provide calming, deep-pressure touch

- Weighted vest (see chapter 9 for directions to make your own)
- Weighted lap desk or lap "snake" (see chapter 9 for directions to make your own)
- Bungee cord bracelets (see chapter 9 for directions to make your own)

Equipment for the Classroom

- Padded chairs
- Theraband leg wraps on chair legs (child can kick for deep proprioceptive input)
- Alternative floor-time seating (e.g., water pillows, beanbag chairs, laundry baskets, balls stabilized in inner tubes or tires, rocking chair, rocker board)
- Water bottles or other mouth toy opportunity

Program/Schedule Changes

- Additional opportunities to move around
- More **doing** than **listening**
- **Arrangements to leave the room in a non-punative way** (e.g., teacher has prearranged with the office to accept an envelope delivered by the child at any time; tasks allow the child to feel helpful, provide calming movement and allow a break from the possible sensory overload of the busy classroom)
- Relaxation strategies

Chapter 8

Suggested Activities for Sensory Diets

This chapter contains a number of multi-sensory activities to provide tactile, vestibular, and proprioceptive sensations during play. All of these activities have been used very successfully with children with PDD. Some recommendations are traditional games all children like to play. Others have been specifically developed for children with PDD, taking into consideration possible problems with comprehension, sensory integration, motor planning, motivation, and attention.

We strive to provide easy, low-cost ideas and try to ensure practicality for parents, teachers, and daycare providers. Activities work best in environments that offer structure and routine. Activities are organized into the following sections

1. Tactile Activities

- General Tactile Activities
- Learning to Feel with Fingers
- Recipes for Tactile Play
- Vestibular Activities
- Proprioceptive Activities

2. Oral Motor (Mouth) Activities

- Learning to Drink from a Straw
- Learning to Blow
- Learning to Chew
- Keeping Mouths Busy
- Learning to Keep Your Chin Dry

3. Fine Motor Activities

- Edible Fine Motor Fun
- Edible Dough
- Homemade Silly Putty

4. Gross Motor Activities

- Swimming Games
- Backyard and Mini-Trampoline Games
- Visual Strategies for Gross Motor Activities

Please consider possible allergies when using food items or sensory materials.

1. Tactile Activities

General Activities

Tactile activities can be an important part of a sensory diet or a fine motor skill-building program. Hand and finger awareness, fine motor planning, and attention can also be developed with the use of tactile activities.

- **Brushing**–varied brushes, drawing with soap crayons or chalk on body and erasing with various textures
- **Massage/back rubs**–varied lotions, powders
- **Tactile adventure bins**–cornmeal, oatmeal, water, sand, lentils
- **Treasure hunt**–hide small objects in Play-Doh® or tactile bin to find with fingers *(no peeking!)*
- **Play-Doh**–see recipes for edible and homemade silly putty
- **Painting**–outdoors with water, paint roller in bathtub, soap crayons
- **Bath time**–bubble bath, crayon soap, back scrub brushes
- **Foam soap or shaving cream**–draw, blow
- **Edible painting**–pudding, yogurt, or applesauce on a tray, put a paper on top to make a "print"
- **Feelie bag, box, or book**–collect small items and different textures to match and sort
- **Kitchen time**–mixing, tasting, smelling, washing up
- **Pet case**–grooming, petting
- **Forts/hideouts**–pillows, scarves, blankets and a flashlight
- **Dress up**–keep a box with gloves, shoes, hats, scarves
- **Make up**–face and body paints, temporary tattoos, or stickers
- **Blindfold games**–Pin the Tail on the Donkey, Blind Man's Bluff (**caution, this may be scary for some children!**)
- **Feelie road**–small carpets, bath mats, rubber mat, sleeping bags
- **Sticky play**–tape, contact paper

Learning to Feel with Fingers

The sense of touch is necessary for manipulation of objects by the hands and fingers. Three-year-old children can usually identify familiar objects by feel and do not need vision to know which of their fingers has been touched or where they have been hurt. The ability to perform precise finger movements, necessary for a task like fastening buttons, depends on feedback about where the button is on the finger tips. Therefore, most children who have poor touch discrimination will have difficulty with many fine motor tasks.

Some children with sensory integration dysfunction constantly touch and manipulate objects. They may mouth objects without being aware of it (Fisher, et al. 1991).

These children may seek additional tactile input because they are hyposensitive to touch sensations.

Do not use light-touch activities for children with tactile defensiveness. Some children enjoy light touch, but others may find it disorganizing and overwhelming even if they are not tactile-defensive. Stop activities if the child is resisting or not actively participating.

Keep in mind when providing tactile activities to pair potentially uncomfortable activities with firm pressure or proprioceptive input to help increase feedback about touch.

- **Tactile adventure bins**–Use large plastic bins or wading pools. Fill these with a variety of textures. If the child still puts things to his mouth, use water, oatmeal, cornmeal, Jell-O® or pudding. Older children will enjoy pouring and sifting sand, rice, lentils, or beans.

- **High fives** (quick and noisy slapping of one hand with another)–Use this whenever giving praise for a job well done. (Can also be used for social interactions like greeting, saying goodbye, etc.)

- **Building hand towers**–Have child lay his hand down, cover with your hand, place child's other hand on top, cover with your other hand, and then show the child how to pull out the bottom hand quickly. Repeat!

- **"One Potato, Two Potato"**–Have children make fists and try the old classic pounding game.

- **Texture books**–Most children with PDD are very interested in books, so combine this interest with a sensory discrimination task. Making a tactile book is easy. Collect samples of contrasting textures. A favourite for young children is an "Old McDonald" book. On each page, cut an animal shape out of a different fabric and be sure to alternate the feel (e.g., rough then smooth, hard then soft, etc.) on subsequent pages. Use sturdy cardboard and glue down the fabric edges with coloured glue. Hole punch the pages and use large rings to hold them together.

Sample pages may include

pig	burlap
chick	feathers
horse	suede leather
cat	sandpaper
cow	spots of felt
duck	terry cloth and silk *(pool of water)*
goose	feathers
grass, sun, etc.	velvet, netting, plastic, canvas

Older children will enjoy a texture book with labels to read (e.g., sandpaper is rough, etc.).

- **Guessing games**–The adult rubs the child's fingers individually (using different textures) and has the child guess which finger or texture was used.
- **Songs**–Consult any preschool resource book for songs and activities. During the song, present different tactile toys like vibrating bugs, loofah sponges, different bath brushes, feather dusters, etc.
- **Finger tugs and hugs**–Adults can provide deep tactile input by grasping each of the child's fingers firmly and drawing down along each finger. Singing "One Little, Two Little, Three Little Fingers," or "Where is Thumbkin?" works well. Older children can learn to do this themselves.
- **Sticky fingers**–Use upside-down contact paper or double-sided carpet tape fastened on a surface. Children love to place their hands (and feet!) on this. Young children may like masking tape stuck to them where they can easily get it off.
- **Tactile bag**–Put bits of fabric and small toys into a cloth bag. Some children love the surprise factor of reaching in a bag and choosing items. Other children who are more tactile defensive may need to see what they are touching.

Recipes for Tactile Play

When introducing these activities, the child may have strong reactions to certain tactile input. If the child is not enjoying the feel of the material, it will not be very motivating or meaningful. Sometimes, adapting the temperature or amount of wetness is all it takes to have the child tolerate it. You can also provide tools such as tongs, spoons, and shovels if finger avoidance is evident. If none of these adaptations make the activity tolerable to the child, simply encourage her to watch. Try the new material at least fifteen times. The goal is to increase acceptance of a greater range of materials or "widening sensory windows" (Wilbarger, 1998).

The following activities are not suitable for children who still persist in mouthing everything. Refer to the Edible Dough and Edible Fine Motor sections for alternate ideas.

Smelly Play-Doh

Combine 2 cups flour with ¼ cup salt, 1 package Kool-Aid®, and 2 tsp. cream of tartar. Then add 1-½ T. oil. Gradually add 1 cup boiling water to the mixture. It will be sticky because it is hot. Let it cool, knead, and add more flour if needed. It keeps for several weeks in the refrigerator in a plastic container or about a week in the open air.

Bubble Mixture

Mix ¼ cup dishwashing liquid with ½ cup water, and 1 tsp. sugar. Add a few drops of food colour if desired. Start with bubble pipes or straws if your child has trouble rounding the lips and blowing with the regular bubble wand.

Salt Dough

Mix 2 cups flour, 1 cup salt, and 1 cup cold water (food colouring optional for colour). Knead mixture until it forms smooth dough. Add more flour or coloured water to reach desired consistency. Dries well in the air. Try a garlic press for great "spaghetti" or monster hair.

Magic Mud

Mix cornstarch with a little water and food colour. Do not worry, as it does not stay together. Let kids run their cars through the "mud." When dry, it vacuums up.

Drizzle Goo

Mix 1 cup flour with ¼ cup sugar, ¼ cup salt, and ¾ cup water with food colour. Place in a squeeze bottle. Great for tactile letters for name cards! Let it dry flat overnight.

Super Simple Sparkle Chalk

Mix a thick paste of white sugar and water, dip sidewalk chalk in paste, and then use on paper. It dries great for tactile numbers and letters (and it lasts). Kids will need help.

Shaving Cream/Foam Soap/Whipping Cream Paint

Easy as pressing the button on the can! Works well on mirrors, windows, or the tub.

Vestibular Activities

Vestibular stimulation can have a significant impact on the nervous system. Quick movements tend to be alerting, and slow movements tend to be calming. Vestibular sensations also help the nervous system stay organized and balanced. All these activities must be supervised carefully! Watch for signs of overload. You may not always immediately see the response, as it can build up over time. Development of the sensory diet should be done slowly and conservatively with the supervision of an experienced occupational therapist.

Negative Responses—Be Aware of These Possibilities

- Excessive yawning, hiccupping, or sighing
- Irregular breathing
- Colour change, face pallor
- Sweating
- Motor agitation
- Increased anxiery
- Pupil dilation
- Changes in sleep/wake patterns
- Significant changes in arousal level (e.g., falling asleep or giddiness)

If the child shows any signs of distress, stop immediately and determine the cause of the child's reactions.

Vestibular Activities

- **Bouncing**–large balls, old mattress
- **Swinging**–in blankets, hammock, toddler swing, playgrounds
- **Spinning**–on swivel chair, Sit 'n Spin, scooter board, tire swing
- **Rocking**–rocking horse, rocking chair
- **Climbing**–playground climbers, ladders, designated furniture
- **Riding toys**–trikes, bikes, scooters, inline skates
- **Walking/running/hiking/swimming**
- **Upside down**–off couch, off lap, on monkey bars, trapeze
- **Roughhousing/wrestling/swinging** while someone pushes on legs
- **Outdoor play**–slides, teeter-totter, roller coaster
- **Recess games**–hopscotch, ball catch, soccer, hockey, tag, etc.
- **Calming vestibular**–slow, rhythmic, linear swinging or rocking; gentle, slow spinning in one direction; gentle bouncing; head-to-heel rocking while on tummy

Proprioceptive Activities

Proprioceptive input can have powerful calming and organizing effects on the nervous system. Necessary precautions are minimal, as this type of sensation is rarely overwhelming. These activities are particularly important to include in sensory diets for children who are sensory defensive. These activities can help to inhibit or prevent uncomfortable reactions to sensations.

- **Stair climbing/sliding**–bumping down on bottom
- **Crawling**–through tunnels or boxes on all fours
- **Playing Tug of War**–with ropes, scarves, stretchy bands
- **Roughhousing**–play wrestling
- **Pulling/pushing**–weighted wagon, wheelbarrow, or cart (weighted)
- **Catching/throwing**–heavy weight ball, beanbags, cushions
- **Kicking**–soccer ball, big ball
- **Carrying heavy items**–groceries, boxes, books
- **Swimming/extra bath time**
- **Big ball activities**
- **Scooter board activities**
- **Silly animal walks**
- **Wheelbarrow walking**
- **Pulling apart resistant toys/objects**–Lego, snap beads, stretchy toys
- **Pounding/rolling**–Play-Doh/clay
- **Hitting**–punching bag or tetherball
- **Squishing between pillows**

- Body stretch
- **Joint compressions**
- **Heavy exercise**–push ups, sit-ups, hand stands, Tug of War, jumping
- **Batting at balls**–use a plastic baseball bat
- **Swinging**–while someone pulls on legs
- **Hanging**–from adult hands or trapeze bar
- **Stirring**–cake batter, pudding, etc.
- **Pushing**–against a wall, another person, hands together
- **Vibration**
- **Gross Motor Activities**–hiking with backpack, biking uphill, obstacle courses, stretching and toning exercises
- **Massage**
- **Biting, chewing, and crunching**–resistive foods or tubing
- **Wearing a weighted vest**

2. Oral Motor Activities

Learning to Drink from a Straw

The ability to drink with a straw is almost essential in our culture. It's convenient and tidy for most families "on-the-go" to throw a juice box in the diaper bag. Sucking also is a calming and organizing activity that requires closing of the lips, lip strength, and the ability to hold the jaw in position. Sucking also uses cheek muscles, helps breathing, and promotes good posture. If the child is having trouble getting started, try a favourite juice box flavor.

You can adapt the straw if needed (find a firmer straw with a wider diameter, like a piece of beverage tubing). Start by dipping the straw into the liquid, placing your finger over the end of the straw, then putting it in the child's mouth. Wait for or assist lip closure, and then release your finger to let the drink go in the mouth. Once the child knows the yummy drink is coming from the straw, place it into the drink box and gently squeeze to make a **small** amount of liquid go up into the straw and be swallowed. Continue gentle squeezes and gradually reduce your help.

If the child does not enjoy any juice box flavors, it is a little more work to find a plastic container with a straw that is squeezable (sports or clear Rubbermaid® type). Again, you may need to shorten the straw. Test it by squeezing the bottle, making the liquid go up the straw easily.

Remember, change is difficult, and many children will resist any new idea. Present the straw several times daily for at least two weeks before deciding the child just is not ready yet!

Increase your child's sucking ability by trying straws of different widths, such as curly straws, use thicker substances, such as apple juice mixed with apple sauce, milkshakes, thinned yogurt, or slushes. Try sucking on firm Jell-O cubes, fruit wedges, Popsicles®, or soup off a spoon.

- **Harmonicas, etc.**–Some whistle-type toys work with air going in and out, so let the child practice alternating these two mouth actions and be the bandmaster!
- Play **"vacuum cleaner"**–Using a straw, suck a piece of coloured lightweight craft foam (about 1" by 1") and move it into a shallow dish. Then, "be the wind" and try blowing it away.

You can increase the child's skills by teaching him to take "big breaths in" (good for relaxation training). Show him how to take and hold a breath by sucking up M&M's® "Minis" or Smarties® at the end of the straw. Challenge the child to pick them up and move as many as possible within twenty seconds—then **eat**!

Learning to Blow

Blowing is excellent for facilitating lip closure, respiration, and breath support for speech, jaw stability, and grading. It helps develop the muscles of the tongue, cheek, jaw, and lips, as well as organize the sensorimotor system. Ask your child to take bigger and longer breaths.

- **Blow bubbles**–in the bathtub with different wands and toys that you can use for bubbles. Many have different mouthpieces that require different mouth positions. Many children who cannot blow bubbles with a regular "bubble wand" do well with a bubble pipe or bubble straw. This provides more support to the lips.
- **Blow toys**–sound makers, party horns, pinwheels, etc.
- **Ping-Pong®** ball table hockey—(Sports-minded kids love this. Sometimes you can find brightly coloured Ping-Pong balls or novelty ones to make it more fun.) Set up barriers on the table like books to mark the "sidelines" and keep balls from flying all over. Make a contest of seeing who can force the ball off their opponent's end of the table.
- Teach her to blow bubbles through the straw into the liquid, (then you have to teach her this is rude!)
- Give him a harmonica and practice alternating inhale/exhale to make different sounds.
- Give her a whistle (best for outside play).
- Use a feather (from a pillow, bird, or craft store), put it in child's hand, and blow it off. If it is too difficult, try a feather on one of those party "blow pipe and ball" toys. Sometimes a feather is easier than the ball as it is lighter and takes less air. Progress to heavier items like Ping-Pong balls, cotton balls, etc.
- Have child blow out candles in various ways. If child does not have good lip protrusion, hold chin in hand and push lips together into pucker. Then

have child breathe out forcefully to blow out one candle. Gradually increase distance and number of candles.

Learning to Chew

Many children with PDD have poor sensory awareness of their mouths and/or low muscle tone, both of which make chewing food more difficult. They may dislike the feel of certain foods, so they do not become good "chewers." All mouth activities will be more successful if the child is in a comfortable and secure position. Make sure his or her feet are supported, and the table is at elbow height.

- A small battery-powered vibrator/massager can be used for a few minutes before the meal to build up muscle tone in the cheeks and tongue (if the child has low tone in these areas).

- Brush the sides of the tongue when you brush your child's teeth. This can help get more tongue movement sideways, which is needed for chewing. An electric toothbrush provides another way to brush the tongue.

- Provide a lot of sensory stimulation to the insides of the cheeks with a toothbrush or by pushing outward on the inside of the cheeks with your fingers.

- Chewing is a partnership between the tongue and the cheeks. Often poor chewing coordination is caused by cheeks that are inactive.

- A "chew stick" is a Popsicle stick with the end wrapped in gauze and dipped in orange juice, grape juice, etc. (something the child likes). The child chews the end to get the flavour.

- A "chew treasure" is a bundle of something yummy tied in a small gauze square with a sturdy string attached. Moisten the gauze, place the "treasure" on the child's molars, and ask her to chew it up to taste the "treasure." Favorites are juicy foods (oranges, apples, sticky caramels, string cheese, etc.) This helps the child keep the food on the molars where it should stay for chewing, and prevents the food from dropping back to the centre of the tongue. With both the chew stick and the chew treasure you may need to place it in her mouth and move the jaw passively for her until she begins to make the motion on her own. (Morris and Klein, 1987).

Keeping Mouths Busy

Why keep mouths busy? Williams and Shellenberger (1994) in their book, *How Does Your Engine Run? A Leader's Guide to the Alert Program for Self-Regulation*, suggest that oral motor input is necessary for the organization of the nervous system. Oetter, Richter, and Frick (1993) in their book, *M.O.R.E.: Integrating the Mouth with Sensory and Postural Functions*, stress the importance of oral motor stimulation in regulating attention and mood. Both of these publications are excellent resources.

- See previous pages for activities to promote blowing, sucking and chewing.
- **Brushing** with a toothbrush, NUK® brush (soft rubber bristles made by Gerber), an infant toothbrush that fits on your finger ("infadent"), toothette, or washcloth

- **Licking** ice cream, Popsicles, lollipops, stickers, or stamps
- **Sweet tastes** are generally calming (sugarless candy, licorice)
- **Sour tastes** are more alerting (sour candy, Popsicles, lemonade)
- **Spicy, bitter foods** are most alerting (taco sauce, cinnamon hearts)
- **Frozen or cold foods** are alerting (frozen grapes, ice chips, Popsicles)
- **Vibration** can be an alerting and organizing input; use electric toothbrushes, vibrating teething toys, or small battery massagers

Learning to Keep Your Chin Dry

A wet chin (or drool) is a frequent concern for children with PDD. Excessive drooling may be a bother to the child and socially awkward. Children with PDD may drool because of sensory processing problems. If a child is a persistent mouth breather and has a chronic mouth open posture, he has incomplete lip closure. This decreases the ability to produce the negative pressure required to adequately suck liquid onto the tongue. Often children with respiratory, upper airway allergies, or sinus problems have open mouth postures, so these problems should be addressed.

Other sensory-related causes include

- Decreased sensitivity in the mouth and subsequently delayed swallow. (If the child does not feel the pooling of saliva, he does not get the message to swallow.)
- Decreased tactile sensation of wet versus dry. Many children who drool do not have this sensory discrimination because they are **always** wet around their chin or lips. If we can keep a child's chin and lips dry as much as possible, the child may begin to notice wetness as she now has something to compare it to. She may initiate wiping her wet chin herself.

Here are some activities to help develop a dry chin

- If the family members, teachers, or mediators are willing, try to keep the child's chin dry for a minimum of two weeks. Always have a dry towel, tennis wristbands, or a cotton bandanna available. Use firm patting, not wiping, to soak up the wetness. You may need to check very frequently to begin with, and then increase the time periods between checks as the child becomes more aware.
- Point out the dry chin, and use **wet** and **dry** words to comment. Point out the dryness while letting the child see her face in a mirror.
- Reinforce the concepts of **wet** versus **dry** in pretend play with puppets or dolls.
- Use verbal or visual cues to increase the child's awareness of the wetness. This can evolve into a routine that trains the child to monitor his chin and swallow the saliva that pools in the mouth. Tennis wristbands (one on each wrist) can be used to wipe the chin and also act as a visual reminder to think about swallowing. Direct the child with words or pictures when his chin is wet to wipe with each hand and then swallow: "wipe, wipe,

swallow" routine. A prearranged wipe signal from the adult or visual cue card may also work.

- If the child's swallow sequence doesn't seem to be effective, practice by squirting small amounts of liquid into the side of her mouth. Tell her you are the mommy elephant feeding her baby or some other silly story depending on the child's age. Use a juice box, squirt toy, or syringe for the elephant's trunk. Squirt, swallow, squirt, swallow. Let her have a turn squirting.

3. Fine Motor Activities

Many children with PDD have significant fine motor delays. These delays may be related to impaired sensory integration. If tactile defensiveness is present, children also will avoid the very activities they need to practice with their fingers, thus contributing to delays. Here is a list of our favourite fine motor activities.

- **Spray bottles and squirt guns** to develop the skill side of the hand
- **Tongs** for pre-scissors skills
- **Squeeze toys** for water and air play
- **Eyedroppers**
- **Spinning tops**
- **Wind-up toys**
- **Two-handed building toys**—Duplo®, Lego, Tinkertoys®, beads, sewing cards
- **Baking**—stirring, rolling, pounding, and pouring
- **Peg boards**
- **Hammer and nails**
- **Bubblewrap**—popping
- **Playing cards**–dealing, counting
- **Pennies in a piggy bank**
- **Puzzles, blocks**
- **Dress-up dolls and action figures**
- **Containers** to open and close for snack time
- **Bingo daubers**, finger paint, paint with water on a chalkboard
- **Computers**
- **Clothes-peg games**
- **Elastic bands**

Edible Fine Motor Fun

Often children with PDD resist "traditional" arts and crafts but may be highly motivated by "treats." Many children will still be using their mouths as a "sensory doorway" (Morris and Klein, 1987), especially if they are very tactile defensive with their fingers. This mouthing behaviour is a challenge, but if the activity promotes tasting and licking, all will enjoy it. The following activities must be supervised carefully. The ideas generally progress from easiest to more difficult. Have fun and happy eating!

Creative (for Visual-Motor Skills)

- **Powder Power**–Lightly sprinkle flour, confectioner's sugar, cocoa, Jell-O, or Kool-Aid powder on a cookie sheet or counter top. Show the child how to draw "roads" or train tracks.

- **Pudding Painting**–Have the child help you make an instant pudding mix or buy the pudding pre-made. Use paper plates to finger paint on—if you use paper, it takes a while to dry before you can display the picture. If you can stand it, have the child lick the fingers for a great oral-motor experience! (Strawberry Cow and Brown Cow syrups dry shiny).

- **Fruit Juice Painting Cubes**–Freeze juice with strong colours (e.g., grape, orange, cranberry) into ice cubes. Use cubes to draw on white paper and pop the rest into cold drinks!

- **Magic Milk Paint**–Open a can of sweetened condensed milk and place in muffin tins. Add a few drops of food colour and paint with Q-Tips®. It dries very shiny.

Two-Handed Tasks (Bilateral Coordination, Finger Dexterity)

- **Cereal Necklaces**–Start threading with O-shaped cereal (Fruit Loops®) onto a pipe cleaner. "Thread one, eat one" works as motivation! Progress to stringing on a licorice string, and then on spaghetti or gimp (craft stores).

- **Opening Skills**–Collect small see-through plastic jars and containers. Carry small cereal or raisin treats with you, but always ask the child to **open** the jar to get inside! Pop-off lids are easiest. Turning comes later and is usually done with the dominant hand. The other hand is the "helper" (or holding hand). Try hand-over-hand help if needed to start and gradually remove your help.

- **Learning to "Spread"**–Use plastic picnic cutlery, wooden tongue depressors, or Popsicle sticks as "knives." Short-handled kid's knives are also good. Large rice crackers or flour tortillas do not break as easily as crackers or bread.

- **Marshmallow Madness**–Gather toothpicks and differently sized marshmallows. Create prickly creatures by poking toothpicks into the marshmallows. You can make theme-based creatures, snowmen, or vehicles.

Edible Dough

Many children are still using their mouths as their "sensory doorway" when we want to begin Play-Doh activities. These recipes offer alternatives that are edible! Provide clean hands and a few tools (theme units are easy to do with cookie cutters). Have fun and happy eating!

Mashed Potato Candy Dough

1 lb. box powdered sugar

2 T. mashed potatoes

2 T. melted margarine or cooking oil (depending on how much tasting will occur)

1 pkg. coconut (optional)

Few drops of milk, cream, or half-and-half

Combine ingredients with hands. Add more powdered sugar to desired consistency.

Peanut Butter Play Dough

1 C. peanut butter

3 T. brown sugar

1 T. raw oatmeal

1 C. corn syrup

1-½ C. powdered sugar

1-½ C. powdered milk

Mix with hands, adding more sugar or dry milk until you can knead it. Add oatmeal or Rice Krispies® for texture. You can make this dough without the corn syrup; you just have to adjust the dry ingredients "by feel."

Frosting Dough

1 can frosting

1 C. peanut butter (optional)

1-½ C. powdered sugar

Knead with hands, very sticky!

Cinnamon Applesauce Dough

2 C. cinnamon

1 C. applesauce

Add enough flour to get desired consistency. Great for fall themes!

Homemade Silly Putty

Many children love to use silly putty or play dough when learning to pound, roll, squeeze, or cut. Play dough may crumble and is often too "babyish" for older children. This putty can be made very stiff, which makes it ideal for holding it in the other hand to cut. Although it may be harder to snip through with scissors, the "stiffness" provides increased tactile and kinesthetic feedback. This putty works great during imaginative play. Use it to stick things together on a temporary basis. The resistance of the putty helps develop finger strength. This recipe is a low-cost alternative to Silly Putty® but not recommended for children who still put fingers or clay in their mouths! It is fun to make in a group, but you should practice first to get the feel of it.

Silly Putty Recipe

Mix together ½ cup water, ½ cup white glue, and food colouring (blue food colouring seems the least edible color, so it visually discourages kids from putting it in their mouths).

Mix another ½ cup water and 1 tsp. Borax® in measuring cup.

Combine above. Knead until the glue forms a putty-like consistency, adding cornstarch gradually. Keep kneading until it is a solid mass.

Store in any airtight container like plastic eggs, film canisters, or zip lock bags.

A great thing about this homemade silly putty is that you can keep adding cornstarch to make it nice and firm with a soft texture. You can easily squeeze it, and it takes more effort to pull it and break it than most soft putties. Also, the more cornstarch, the less sticky. This recipe makes enough for 8 to 10 children to put it in their "fidget" bags.

Silly Putty Activities

Keep a large plastic tub of putty and dump it on the table with cookie cutters, scissors, rolling pins, etc. Theme-based cookie cutters are easy to find.

Hide small toys or coins in it for finger strength.

For fingertip skills, use thumb and pincer fingers of **one hand only** to roll baby dinosaur eggs or alien eggs (whatever small round eggs fit the play themes). Puppets or clickers held by the other hand "eat" the eggs.

Make "creatures" with toothpicks and putty.

4. Gross Motor Activities

All children benefit from active movement of the large muscles in the arms, legs, and trunk. Exercise of these muscles promotes strength, endurance, posture, balance, and coordination. Participation in gym class and eventual recreation activities are highly dependent on gross motor skills. Children with PDD may be reluctant to practice these activities, especially if the underlying sensory foundation skills are weak. They benefit from routine and easily practiced activities. We have included our favourite gross motor activities.

- Walks and hikes
- Running, skipping, and hopping
- Dancing, marching to music
- Playing ball hockey, soccer, or basketball
- Jumping on a mini-trampoline or trampoline (see trampoline activity sheet)
- Walking on stilts (cans with skipping rope handles) or "big feet"
- Tumbling and wrestling

- Hide-and-Seek
- Playing on the playground
- Bowling
- Ice skating
- Inline skating
- Bike riding or trike riding
- Tether ball
- T-ball
- Hopscotch
- Hoop games
- Racquet sports
- Obstacle courses
- Beanbag/Nerf® ball/Frisbee® catch and throw games
- Track and field
- Big ball games
- Swimming
- Scooter board tag

Swimming Games

Many children with PDD love to swim; perhaps this is because it is such a total sensory experience. The weight and pressure of the water against the body can be relaxing and increases body awareness. Outdoor pools are generally preferred, due to natural lighting and less noise echoing off hard surfaces. The ability to swim is almost essential for safety in our culture. Many therapy goals are part of a plan because swimming is such a motivating activity.

Get laminated pictures for all your child's favourite swimming songs. Pair the song with the visual aid and the motor actions. You can also put pictures inside plastic bags or clear self-adhesive vinyl covering. Allow the child to make choices of favourite songs/games.

The following songs/activities promote language and provide sensory input

- "Swimming, Swimming in the Swimming Pool" (great actions)
- "Motorboat"—Whirl around on flutter board or holding hands through the water singing "Motorboat, motorboat go so slow! (Kick slowly.) Motorboat, motorboat go so fast! (Speed up.) Motorboat, motorboat step on the gas! (Kick as fast as possible.)"
- "Here We Go Round the Mulberry Bush"–Change the song's words (e.g., this is the way we blow big bubbles, ...kick our feet ...splash our face)
- "The Grand Old Duke of York" (wonderful up and down movement)
- "Ring Around the Rosey"

- "Jack in the Box"–"Sitting so still, won't you come in?" "Yes, I will" (jump into water)
- "Humpty Dumpty" (jump off tube into water)
- "Row, Row, Row Your Boat" (use air mattress or flutter board)
- "Five Green and Speckled Frogs" (jump into the water)
- "Scrub, Scrub, Scrub Our Sillies Out" (tune: "Shake Our Sillies Out;" use therapy brush)
- "Hokey Pokey" (may persuade a reluctant child to put a face, foot, or hand in)
- Blowing Bubbles–start with straws and show how to blow, gradually cut the straw shorter; blow ping-pong balls across the water; take a small, non-breakable mirror under water to encourage eyes open and bubble blowing

Backyard and Mini-Trampoline Games

A large, backyard trampoline can be a wonderful therapeutic piece of equipment the whole family can enjoy. An indoor mini-trampoline is a versatile piece of equipment that involves movement and body awareness and assists in gross motor skill development.

Unfortunately, a trampoline can also be dangerous. It must be set up and supervised carefully. Usually only one person at a time is recommended to be on the trampoline; however, when dealing with children with special needs, this may be unrealistic, and you may require another person to assist the children. A responsible adult can jump safely with a child, providing they don't bounce too high and stay toward the middle of the trampoline.

A heavy adult and light child is the most dangerous combination, and adults should practice the stop bounce maneuver right away (stop jumping, bend knees, and absorb the bounce, balancing with your hands out if needed). This "stop" should also be taught to the child, perhaps with a visual cue such as a stop sign or red circle that represents a red traffic light.

An indoor mini-trampoline is generally a safe piece of equipment if basic rules are followed, such as only one person allowed on the trampoline at a time, keep away from sharp or hard furniture, and provide hand support, if needed, to begin.

The following activities progress from easiest to more difficult

- Sit and hold hands and sing "Bouncing Up and Down on The Big Trampoline" (sung to the tune of Raffi's "Bouncing Up and Down in My Little Red Wagon") or "Row, Row, Row Your Boat" while rocking back and forth and gently bouncing.
- Knee bouncing–let the child hold your hands in a face-to-face position.

- Standing up–(same as above) holding hands or turning the child away from you. Provide deep pressure by squeezing with your legs while you sing or count and rhythmically bounce. Have another adult watch the child's face for signs of distress. Most children find this position very secure and love it!

- Bumper car–once child is comfortable running around, introduce "crashing" and falling in a safe, controlled manner. Bump with your shoulders or back, arms crossed, no pushing allowed.

- "Ring Around the Rosey"–after you all fall down, be sure to include the child pulling you up as part of the game! Make a big fuss of "Help, help– pull me up!" The pulling builds interactions skills as well as providing good organizing sensory input.

- "Humpty Dumpty Sat on the Ball" (bring ball to sit on). The trampoline is a safe and fun place to practice falling.

- Racetrack–use colored circles of construction paper for red/green "traffic lights" or use a homemade **Stop** sign. Practice jumping/running and stopping on command.

- Jumping like various animals–use picture cues at end of this chapter.

- Drops–seat drops, knee drops, doggy drops (on hands and knees)

- Rolling games–roll across and over each other, singing "There were ten in the bed and the little one said, 'I'm tired, roll over…'" Monitor this vestibular input carefully because it can be over-stimulating for sensitive children.

- Tag games–chase and catch

Visual Strategies for Gross Motor Activities

Sensory-motor activities or total body activities that demand heavy work are often recommended. They are recognized for the organizing effect they have on the nervous system. However, many of these activities are difficult to teach a child with PDD due to communication barriers and difficulty with motor planning. Hodgdon (1995) has found visual aids to be an effective strategy for children with auditory processing and communication problems.

Many picture symbols are now available (such as Boardmaker™ by Mayer Johnson), but there is a lack of appropriate pictures for sensory-motor activities. We have included visual aids to assist children's participation in some specific gross motor activities.

Shirley Sutton, one of the authors of this book, and Marion Foubert, illustrator, developed these visual aids. In our experience, pictures are helpful during OT programs because they aid children's comprehension, enhance sequential skills, and improve attention to tasks. We have also found children to be more cooperative when they have visual preparation for upcoming changes in the activity program.

By using picture sequences that are stable over time, the children learn the "game" and will often make choices of preferred "games." Making therapy "exercises" more interactive enhances learning and motivation. In fact, self-directed activity is considered crucial to motor planning in traditional sensory integration theory (Ayres, 1975).

We use line drawings because they are less distracting than photographs. The drawings were set up to be customized for your child by cutting out favourites and placing them into a standard, small photo album. Using these visual aids, or making your own, is well worth the effort! Watch for immediate results with many children in the areas of comprehension, transitioning, and compliance.

Pictures also help parents and teachers define a beginning and end to an activity and to quickly and easily begin therapy programs. Quill (1995) also notes that concrete picture cues are invaluable aids that help children with PDD deal with last minute changes of plans or deviations from routine.

Examples of Four Main Types of Activities

"Roughhousing" or physical games. These activities feature face-to-face interaction and foster your child's attention span and interaction skills. Communication skills, as well as sensory and motor skills, are encouraged as you have fun together. Use your child's love of movement and deep-pressure touch sensation to foster interactive games. Using a familiar song over and over with the same "game" is wonderful to reinforce language skills.

Silly animal walks. These challenging positions are excellent for floor time at home, circle times at school, or transition times when children need to move to another spot. The positions provide heavy muscle work, which builds body awareness and helps with motor planning.

Big ball exercises. Big ball activities are often very successful for children as they provide movement input and pressure input, which can be motivating and organizing. These pictures can turn playing on a big ball into a series of games that work on interaction and communication skills, such as turn taking, choice making, requesting help, saying "stop/go," etc. Although therapy balls are available now at most large drug stores, less expensive balls from toy stores are often acceptable. "Hop" balls with handles will also work for these activities—just turn the handles out of the way.

Scooter board activities. The pictures provide ideas for this common piece of therapy equipment (see equipment in chapter 9 for information on how to build your own). Scooter board activities are used for movement and body awareness, as well as foundation motor skills like back extension, sitting posture, arm and neck strength, and muscle tone.

Roughhousing Games

Yankee Doodle Went to Town...

Objective
- To provide touch pressure to child's tummy area
- To provide linear calming movement
- To develop "protective reactions" in arms when you lower them to the ground

Grand Old Duke of York

Objectives
- To provide movement, paired with language, up and down
- To increase body position sense and head movement
- To develop adult's upper body strength!

Start with small lifts until child is comfortable.

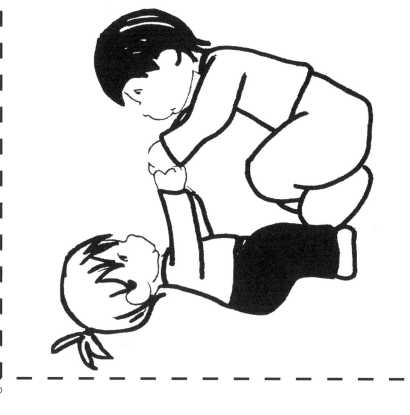

Row, Row, Row Your Boat

Objectives
- To provide firm pressure touch to hands
- To increase body awareness through push-pull activity
- To develop upper body strength
- To promote standing balance

Up and Over

Objectives
- To provide strong head movement in the upside-down position
- To develop arm and hand strength

Be sure the child has good muscle tone before trying—use another adult to "spot."

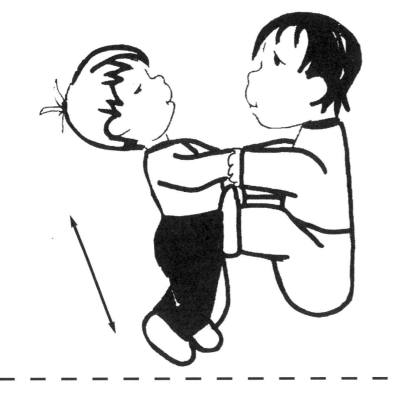

Airplane Ride

Objectives
- To provide deep pressure touch to hands and tummy
- To increase body awareness through up, down, sway
- To develop back and neck extension muscles
- To promote basic balance

Teddy Bear—Climb the Stairs

Objectives
- To provide deep-pressure touch to hands
- To increase body awareness and standing balance
- To develop standing balance

You may adapt the same chant to a variety of motor movements.

Boat Ride

Objectives
- To provide deep-touch pressure to body
- To provide calming head movement
- To promote language skills

Chant: "Rock the boat 'til we laugh and shout, rock the boat 'til we all fall out!"

Trot, Trot Trolley Horse

Objectives
- To provide deep-pressure input to child's tummy
- To develop "protective reactions" in arms when you "shake them off"

Chant "Trot, trot trolley horse up and down; look out [child's name], don't fall down!

Push-Pull

Objectives
- To provide calming push-pull input without direct touch (especially good for sensory-defensive children)
- To increase body awareness through push-pull activity
- To develop upper body and handgrip strength

Head Down

Objectives
- To provide head upside-down position (strong vestibular)
- To increase eye tracking

Song idea: "Ring Around the Rosey" (We all fall down)

Silly Animal Walks

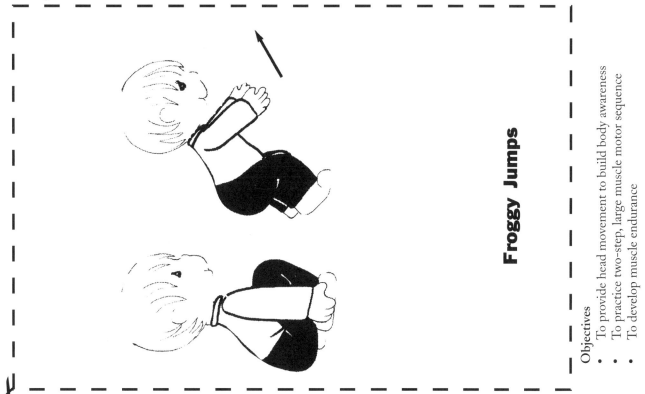

Froggy Jumps

Objectives
- To provide head movement to build body awareness
- To practice two-step, large muscle motor sequence
- To develop muscle endurance

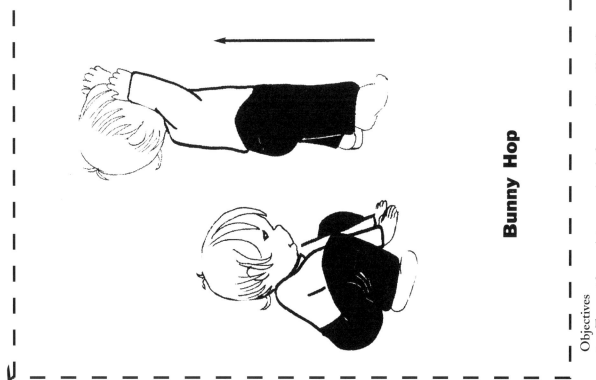

Bunny Hop

Objectives
- To provide touch input to hands from pushing off the floor
- To build strength in legs
- To develop two-sided body coordination
- To promote two-step motor sequence

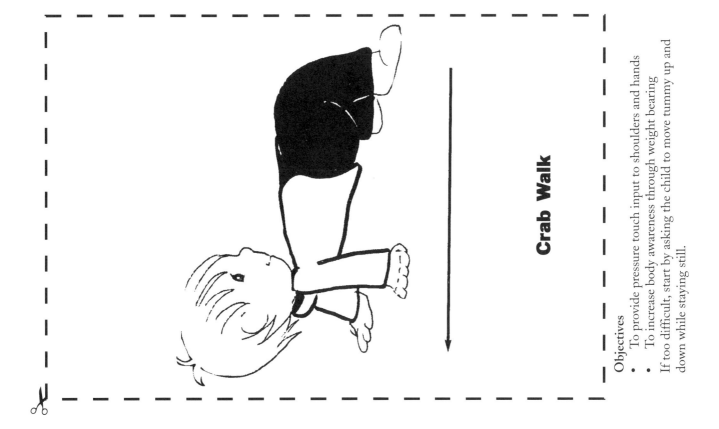

Crab Walk

Objectives
- To provide pressure touch input to shoulders and hands
- To increase body awareness through weight bearing

If too difficult, start by asking the child to move tummy up and down while staying still.

Bear Walk

Objectives
- To provide tactile desensitization to hands from weight bearing on the floor
- To increase body awareness

Requires complex coordination of two body sides.

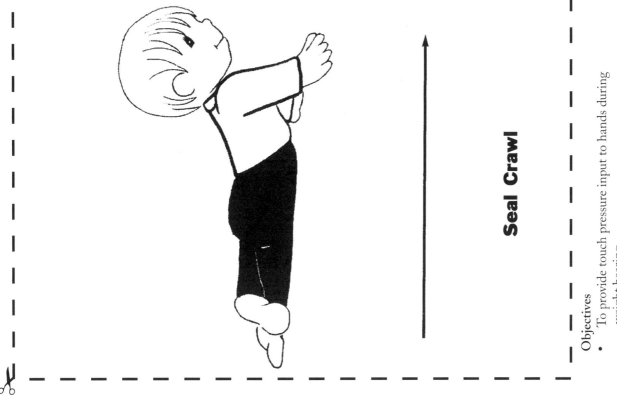

Seal Crawl

Objectives
- To provide touch pressure input to hands during weight bearing
- To increase upper back extension strength
- To build arm strength

Turtle Crawl

Objectives
- To provide touch input to back from carrying an object
- To increase body awareness
- To develop upper body strength
- To promote motor control by moving fast versus slow

Bottom Slide

Objectives
- To provide touch pressure input to hands from floor
- To increase body awareness
- To provide calming input from demanding heavy work from hip, tummy, and arm muscles

Big Ball Section

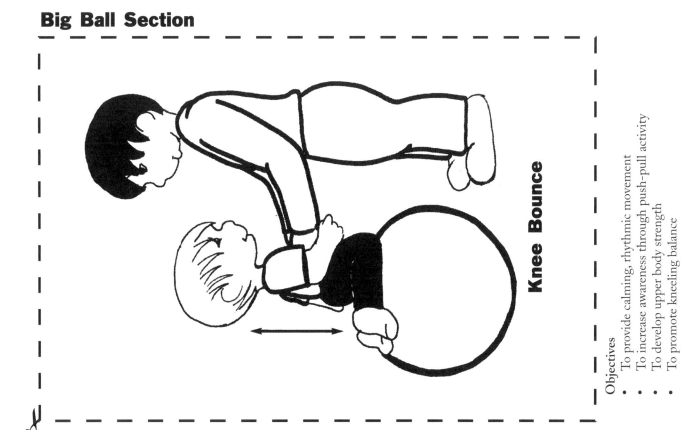

Knee Bounce

Objectives
- To provide calming, rhythmic movement
- To increase awareness through push-pull activity
- To develop upper body strength
- To promote kneeling balance

through Sensory Integration

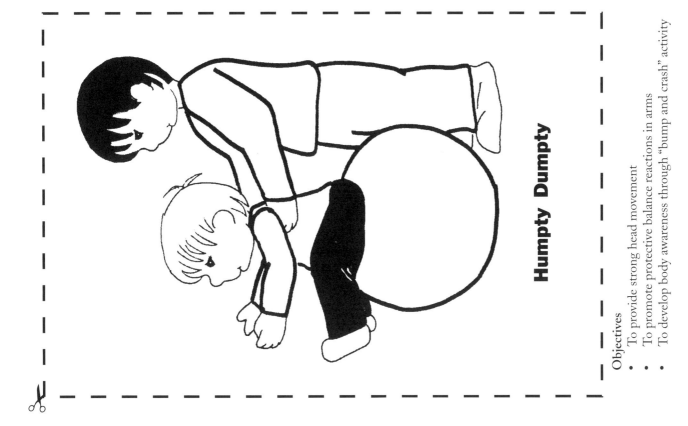

Humpty Dumpty

Objectives
- To provide strong head movement
- To promote protective balance reactions in arms
- To develop body awareness through "bump and crash" activity

Ball Kick

Objectives
- To increase awareness of legs and feet
- To develop one-foot standing balance
- To promote eye-foot coordination

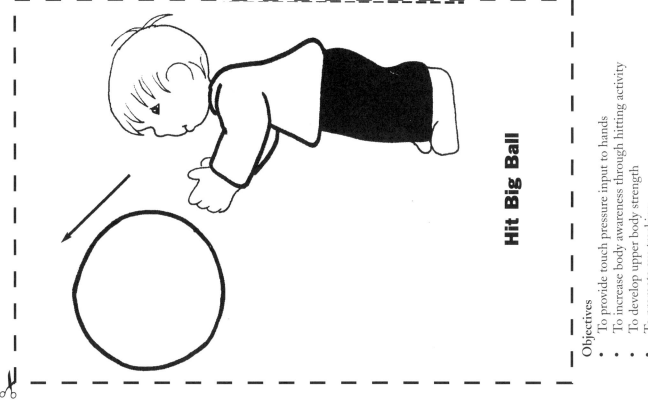

Hit Big Ball

Objectives
- To provide touch pressure input to hands
- To increase body awareness through hitting activity
- To develop upper body strength
- To promote eye tracking

Tummy Throw

Objectives
- To provide touch pressure to body from floor
- To increase back and neck extension strength
- To develop arm strength
- To develop good eye tracking (roll ball)

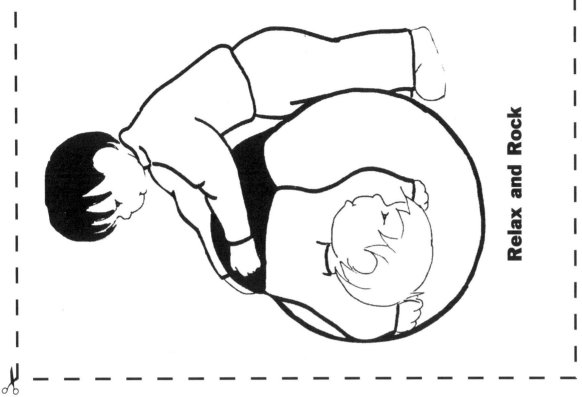

Relax and Rock

Objectives
- To provide slow, boring rhythmic movement for calming
- To promote relaxation through the head down position
- To increase tactile contact with tummy and face
- To promote simple balance skills

Tummy On Ball

Objectives
- To increase movement input
- To promote back and neck extension muscle strength
- To promote protective movement reactions in arms and legs
- To develop simple balance skills

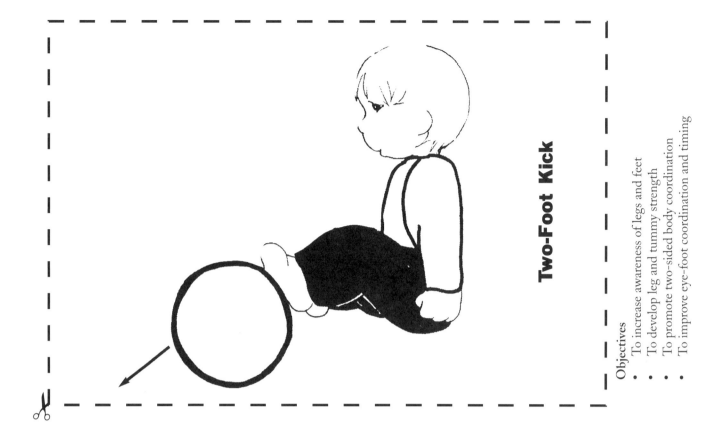

Two-Foot Kick

Objectives
- To increase awareness of legs and feet
- To develop leg and tummy strength
- To promote two-sided body coordination
- To improve eye-foot coordination and timing

Sit and Bounce

Objectives
- To provide up and down head movement
- To increase body awareness through hips and feet
- To promote sitting balance
- To build rhythm and counting skills

Push Big Ball

Objectives
- To provide touch pressure to hands
- To provide calming heavy muscle work
- To build strength in wrists and arms

(Note to adult: stand opposite child and provide resistance.)

Scooter Board Section

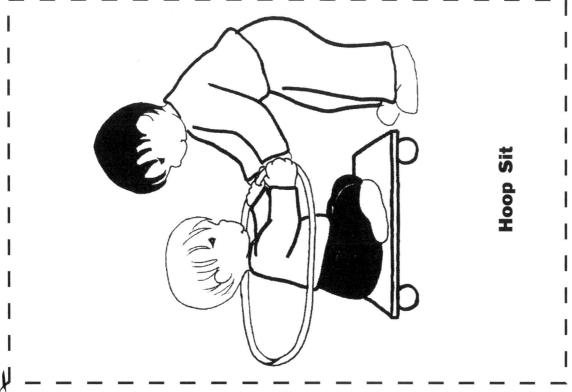

Hoop Sit

Objectives
- To provide touch pressure to hands from holding hoop
- To increase body awareness
- To develop upper body strength
- To promote sitting balance
- To increase body awareness through push-pull activity

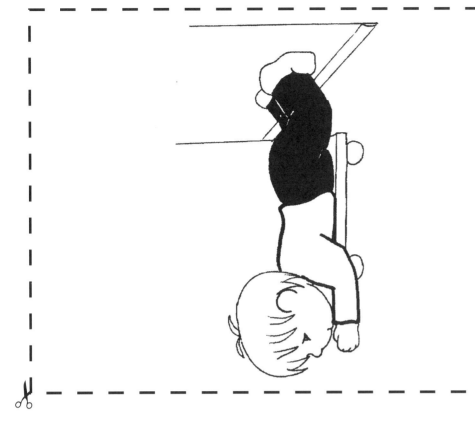

Rocket "Blastoff" with Feet

Objectives

• To develop strong back and hip extension
• To develop the muscle sense in legs and feet
• To promote sense of timing (countdown to "blastoff")
• To provide fast movement (acceleration)

Knee Ride

Objectives

• To provide touch pressure to hands when holding hoop
• To increase body awareness through push–pull activity
• To develop upper body strength
• To promote kneeling balance

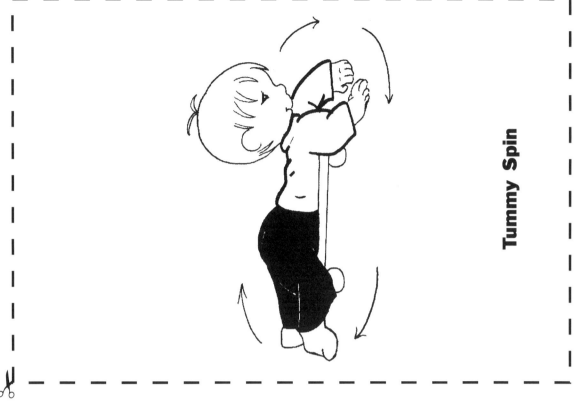

Tummy Spin

Objectives

- To develop strong back and neck extension muscles
- To develop arm and shoulder strength
- To promote motor planning–start/stop/change direction, and rotational movement
- To promote crossing the midline of the body with arms

Rocket "Blastoff" with Hands

Objectives

- To provide heavy muscle work for shoulders and wrists
- To promote sense of timing (countdown to "blastoff")
- To provide fast head movement (acceleration)
- To promote movement without vision (going backwards)

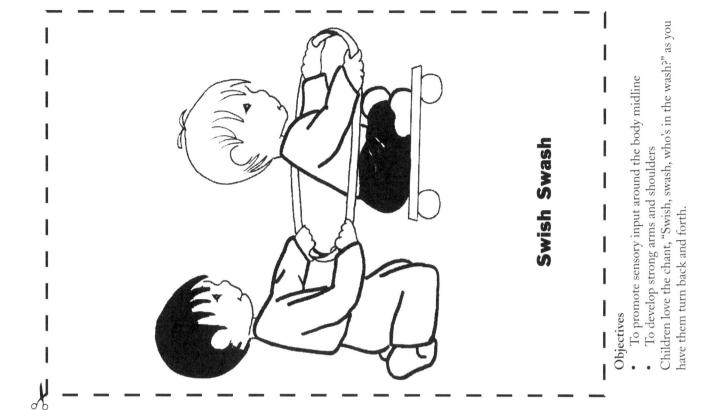

Swish Swash

Objectives
- To promote sensory input around the body midline
- To develop strong arms and shoulders

Children love the chant, "Swish, swash, who's in the wash?" as you have them turn back and forth.

Chapter 9

Equipment and Resources

This chapter contains a number of instructions for making equipment that we have found helpful in our experience working with children with PDD. Often parents, schools, and childcare centres don't know where to find equipment or do not have the resources to purchase the equipment from specialty catalogues.

By providing easy and low-cost instructions or purchasing sources, children will have access to the sensorimotor experiences they need. All of these suggestions are very adaptable to your child's size, body weight, and personal preferences. A brief explanation of how and why to use the specific equipment is included.

The resources are organized into the following sections

1. "Make-It-Yourself" Equipment Ideas
   - Weighted Vest
   - Chewy Bungee Cord Bracelet
   - Platform Swing
   - Stress Balloon Fidget Toy
   - Low-Cost, Indoor Sensory Equipment Ideas
   - Weighted Lap Snake
   - Scooter Board
   - Fidget Bag Toys
2. Resources
   - Suppliers
   - Videos
   - Books
   - Websites

1. Make-It-Yourself Equipment Ideas

Weighted Vest

The idea of a vest providing calming, deep-pressure input comes from a famous adult with autism—Temple Grandin. She finds that certain children who fidget all the time will often be calmer when given a padded, weighted vest to wear. She herself was greatly calmed by pressure. Williams (1996) feels padded clothing protects her highly sensitive tactile system from too much sensation. There is no scientific research that explores the use of a weighted vest. In our clinical experience, children who constantly seek deep-touch pressure, are sensory defensive, and are easily distracted (or who have poor body awareness) benefit from the extra weight the vest provides.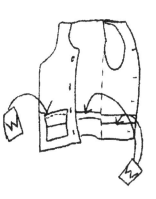

The vest is custom-made to fit the child snugly in a comfortable fabric that the child prefers. It is padded and weighted to a maximum of no more than ten percent of the child's body weight.

The weighted vest should be worn for approximately twenty minutes and then removed for a few minutes, as this prevents the nervous system from adapting to the new sensation of increased weight. However, if the child has difficulty with the tactile input of putting the vest on and taking it off, the vest may be worn longer. Other children simply use their vest for work times at their desk, as it helps them sit quietly. There is no hard and fast rule. Feel free to experiment and discuss it with your OT.

If you want to try this strategy before someone commits to sewing or purchasing a vest, a bag of rice in the child's backpack or fanny pack may give him or her the idea. Ask your OT if she has a vest you may borrow for a few weeks. Discuss the schedule for wearing it with the family or school.

Instructions for Sewing

If you are lucky, you may find a sturdy, new or used vest with buttons or snaps that fits the child. Alternatively, sew one from a child's pattern. Fabrics such as fleece, denim, and corduroy seem to work well and can withstand machine washing! When choosing a fabric, also consider summer weather and whether the child will be wearing the vest mainly indoors or outdoors.

Try the vest on the child and consider where you intend the weight to be. Typical placements are below the shoulder blades, on the upper chest, and close-in around hip level. You need to create "pockets" for the weights to sit in. The weights can be simple ziplock sandwich bags filled with sand or rice, round flat washers, or vertical blind drapery weights. Be aware of the safety risk if the child gets into things and still eats non-edibles.

1. Decide what you are going to use for weights and make the pockets accordingly. Use sturdy fabric for the pockets or pad the pockets so the child will not feel the weights moving around. Three vertical-blind weights (or 2.5 oz. non-lead fishing weights) sewn into small "packets" make approximately ½ pound per packet. Most pre-school children start with twleve-to-twenty-four weights, which will total two-to-four pounds.

2. Sew pockets snugly to fit the weights and distribute the weights evenly. Often you need to put a small piece of Velcro at the top of each pocket to ensure the weights do not shift. Remove or add weights to adjust; sometimes, the child accepts the vest better if the weights are added gradually. When washing the vest, remember to remove the weights.

Weighted Lap Snake

Many children with PDD find sitting still for any reason very difficult due to their sensory needs. Extra weight provides deep-pressure touch and calming proprioceptive input. Many children cannot tolerate a weighted vest, but they may tolerate a less intrusive "lap snake." This is an easy way to try the concept and see how the child responds.

Sew one or more snakes and introduce them when the child is sitting–calm and happy. Place one (or more) in the child's lap or drape it over his shoulders. Observe if the child is less restless. Some teachers use the weighted snakes as substitutes when they cannot stay right beside the child.

Instructions for Sewing

1. Find long tube socks, one for each "snake." Alternatively, use thick tights or stockings and cut them off about 18" from the toe. Serge or whipstitch the cut edges.

2. Fill each sock with four cups of rice or other similar pellets like pinto beans or spilt peas.

3. Close the end of the tube sock by hand or machine, sewing the opening with small, sturdy stitches.

4. If desired, draw a simple face on the sewn side of the sock, making the seam the "mouth."

Stress Balloon Fidget Toy

As part of a sensory diet or sensory activity program, many children need extra touch input. This balloon toy is squeezable, which provides the child a chance to use calming, deep-pressure touch while using the toy. The toy is very quiet. This means it can be used in school, church, or other environments where noise is a factor. The resistance of the balloon is excellent for learning to squeeze and release, as taught in many progressive-relaxation training programs.

Keep the stress toy in a pocket, fanny pack, or fidget basket that can be made available to the child when there is "downtime," or when waiting more than a minute or two is required. It can also be used as a sensory preparation toy where a child squeezes and releases several times to build awareness of finger position before doing a fine motor task like drawing.

Supplies

- Two or three 9" helium-quality balloons
- Filling: flour, lentils, birdseed, or coffee (for added sensory smell input), rice, pinto beans, split peas, or other non-toxic substance
- Plastic pop bottle
- Tiny elastics or fine thread

Instructions

1. Pour about ¼ to ½ cup of filling into a plastic pop bottle.
2. Inflate a balloon to about the size of a fist, pinch the neck, and stretch the neck of the balloon securely over the neck of the bottle.

3. Turn the bottle over. The contents of the bottle should displace the air and pour into the balloon. If not, gently squeeze the bottle.

4. Remove balloon from bottle, squeeze out the excess air, and secure the neck with a tiny elastic or piece of thread. If desired, snip the "lips" of the balloon off first.

5. Cut the neck off a second balloon and stretch it over the first balloon, inserting the sealed end in first (like putting on a bathing cap).

6. If you wish a three-layer balloon, repeat with a third balloon.

Caution: Balloons, if eaten, can be very dangerous for young children. Latex allergies may prevent any balloons in the classroom. If children use the stress balloon near their mouths, look for a more appropriate, and safe, mouth-toy.

Making a Platform Swing

Materials

- Good quality plywood (4' x 2-½')
- Good quality rope (amount depends on the height of your ceiling)
- Pipe insulation (approximtely 14' to go around the edge of the swing)
- Vinyl (approximately 14' to cover the pipe insulation)
- Eight clamps
- Staples
- D-ring (to hang the swing from a beam in the ceiling)

Have a contractor inspect the beams of your ceiling to ensure strength. The eye-bolt inserted into the beam should be welded to prevent stretching of the bolt. A swivel device is recommended to prevent the ropes from twisting over each other.

Complete instructions regarding installation of a swing and equipment are available from Southpaw. Please see Resources at the end of this book.

Instructions

1. Round edges of the plywood and drill two holes in each corner to accomodate the rope.

2. Cut the rope into four equal pieces and string through the holes at each corner. Clamp the ropes (Figure 1).

3. At the other end of each rope, make a loop and clamp it. Ensure each rope is exactly the same length (Figure 2).

4. Staple the pipe insulation around the perimeter of the swing (Figure 3).

5. Staple the vinyl over the top of the pipe insulation (Figure 3).

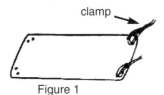

Figure 1   Figure 2   Figure 3

Making a Scooter Board

Materials

- Good quality plywood (2' x 1' or measure from child's armpit to midthigh for appropriate length)
- Padding (carpet under pad works well)
- Vinyl to cover
- Staples
- Four castors (we recommend good quality Shepherd castors)

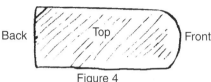

Figure 4

Instructions

1. Cut the plywood and round front corners (Figure 4).
2. Staple the padding onto the board.
3. Staple the vinyl covering over the board.
4. Secure the castors underneath (ensure your screws are not longer than the thickness of your plywood) (Figure 5).

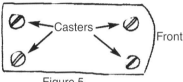

Figure 5

Instruct your children on the safety of the scooter board. It is for sitting and lying prone or supine only.

- **Never Stand on Your Scooter Board**
- **During activities that are fast, a helmet is recommended**
- **Always supervise your child on the scooter board**

Making a Bungee Cord Bracelet

Materials

- Piece of bungee cord (length 1.5 times the circumference of the child's wrist)
- Electrical tape

Instructions

1. Cut the bungee cord to the desired length.
2. Fit it on the child's wrist and tape the ends together with electrical tape.

Low-Cost, Indoor Sensory Equipment Ideas

Many children with PDD have a strong need to move. It helps them keep focused, adaptable, and skillful. Movement opportunities are essential components of sensory diets. Unfortunately, many schools have greatly reduced their indoor and outdoor playground equipment because of costs and safety risks. However, there are many low-cost ways to provide sensory input that children with PDD love and enjoy.

How Do You Use Indoor Equipment?

We explored the link between behaviour and strong sensory needs, especially for vestibular (movement) and proprioceptive (body position sense). This list gives more suggestions for equipment not already discussed.

Equipment Ideas

- Cardboard boxes–for rolling, tunnels, and hideouts
- Blankets and hammocks–for swinging, hiding, and rolling
- Swivel chairs–for spinning (remember to ask the child to direct the activity!)
- Old mattresses/air mattresses, water beds–jump and crash
- Blow-up/plastic wading pools–great sensory bins to fill with rice, beans, or pillows
- A smooth, thin board, eight-to-ten inches wide and several feet long– makes an indoor slide by placing it up steps. You can also make a bridge by putting it across a few books or make a teeter-totter over a flat stool
- Broomsticks or dowel–use to do chin-ups or floor pulls
- Beach balls–fill with small amount of water to make a "wacky ball" that will not run away because the water weighs it down
- Old bicycle inner tubes–for stretching and playing Tug of War
- Laundry baskets–to sit and climb in and out of (good for symbolic play; e.g., train or bus ride)
- Inner tubes–great mini-trampolines
- Zoomball–a great two-person game for upper body coordination and visual tracking. Many children with PDD love this toy because it is highly visual. Attach one set of the handles up high on a hook and let the children send the "buoy" up. Also try it lying down, kneeling, or on tummy. For preschool children, the dollar store version is fine because the strings are shorter.

Fidget Bag Toys

As discussed in chapter 5, many children with PDD find sensory experiences to be soothing and organizing. As adults we all "fidget" with pens, coins, jewelry, etc. Children often need more intense input for the same sensory benefits: keeping awake, alert, and attentive. When teaching use of fidget toys, the long-range goal is self-control and dignity.

When children have fewer "meltdowns," they feel better about themselves and their ability to be in control. Parents and teachers appreciate the chance to go to church, a shopping mall, or a restaurant without worrying about tantrums or odd-looking behaviours. Waiting times and long car or bus rides may be easier if the child can be happily "fidgeting."

Often a basket or bin is kept handy at school, or a fanny pack is used for outings. Items need to be changed frequently because the sensory system adapts, and sensory diets are enriched by new sensory experiences. Provide clear rules for using fidgets toy: keep toys in hand or lap, one toy at a time, return all "fidgets" to the bag or basket. Consult with your occupational therapist for other ideas for mouth and tactile activities, all of which can be included in a "fidget" bag. Of course, if children are still putting things in their mouth, you will need to screen the items for safety.

What should go in a fidget bag? The child's sensory likes and dislikes should be considered, as well as the sensory goals and specific sensory diet. A combination of mouth, tactile, and small finger toys for manipulation is generally preferred. Highly visual toys are not recommended if the fidgets are for group time; they will be too distracting for the other children. Here are some favourites

- Lotion
- Scrub brushes
- Massager or small vibrator
- Scratch 'n sniff stickers
- Stress balls or flour balloon
- Therapy putty, Silly Putty, or other "slime"
- Mouthing toys (e.g., chewy, coffee stir sticks, Nuk brush, infant chew toys, harmonica, blow toys)
- Food items like hard candies, gum, licorice, etc.
- Hair elastics or rubber bands
- Key ring
- Bungee cord bracelets
- Jewelry (e.g., watch bands with Velcro closures, necklaces, bracelets)
- Transformers® or other tiny toys with parts that move
- Mini-spray bottle ("spritzer" with water)
- Stretch toys
- Koosh balls
- Fabric swatches
- Bendables such as small rubber toys, certain hair curlers, pipe cleaners, or twist ties
- Deck of cards

2. Resources

Suppliers

Clipper Mill
PO Box 420376
San Francisco, CA 94142-0376

Tel (415) 552-5005
Fax (415) 552-6296
Email: info@clippermill.com
www.clippermill.com

Distributes surgical brushes, but you need to purchase in bulk.

Flaghouse Special Populations and Rehabilitation
601 Flaghouse Dr.
Hasbrouck Heights, NJ 07604-3116

Tel (800)-743-7900
Email: sales@flaghouse.com
www.flaghouse.com

In Canada:
235 Yorkland Blvd., Suite 300
North York, ON M2J 4Y8 Canada

Tel (800)-265-6900
Email: flaghousecanada@flaghouse.com

Future Horizons, Inc.
721 W. Abram St.
Arlington, TX 76013

Tel (800) 489-0727
Fax (817) 277-2270
International tel. +1-817-277-0707
Email: info@futurehorizons-autism.com
www.FutureHorizons-Autism.com

Worl'd largest publisher of books, videos, CDs, DVDs, and other resources on autism and Asperger's Syndrome. Also sponsors workhops and conferences. Free catalog available.

New Visions—Mealtimes Catalog
1124 Roberts Mountain Rd.
Faber, VA 22938

Tel: (800) 606-3665
Email mealtime@new-vis.com
www.new-vis.com

A resource for oral-motor, feeding and mealtime programs

OT Ideas Inc.
124 Morris Turnpike
Randolph, NJ 07869

Tel (877) 768-4332
Fax (973) 895-4204
E-mail: otideas@otideas.com

Sensory motor toys and therapeutic equipment

PDP Products and Professional Development Programs

14524 61st Street Court North   Tel (651) 439-8865
Stillwater, MN 55082   Fax (651) 439-0421
     Email: Products@pdppro.com
     www.pdppro.com

Sensory and motor toys, equipment, surgical brushes, books, assessment materials, and workshops on topics related to sensory integration

Playaway Toy Company

PO Box 247   Tel (888) 752-9929
Bear Creek, WI 54922   www.playawaytoy.com

Indoor swings that fit easily into any doorway

Pocket Full of Therapy, Inc.

PO Box 174   Tel (800) 736-8124
Morganville, NJ 07751   Email PFOT@PFOT.com
     www.pfot.com

Therapeutic toys, useful for home and school programming, videos

Sensory Resources LLC

2200 E. Patrick Lane, Suite 3A   Tel (888) 357-5867
Las Vegas, NV 89119   Fax (702) 891-8899
     International tel. +1-702-433-0404
     Email: info@SensoryResources.com
     www.SensoryResources.com

Publishes books, videos, CD's, and other resources for parents, teachers, and therapists. Also sponsors workshops and conferences on sensory integration and related topics. Free catalog available.

Southpaw Enterprises

PO Box 1047   Tel (800) 228-1698
Dayton, OH 45401   Fax (937) 252-8502
     International Tel +1-937-252-7676
     Email: therapy@southpawenterprises.com
     www.southpawenterprises.com

Equipment used in sensory integration treatment, including suspended equipment, tactile activities, weighted vests and blankets, therapy balls and other fine and gross motor equipment, books, videos, and toys for use at home and school.

Therapro Inc.
22 Arlington St
Framingham, MA 01702-8732

Tel (800)-257-5376
Fax (508) 875-2062
Email: info@theraproducts.com
www.theraproducts.com

Toys and equipment used in sensory integration treatment and home and school programming, fine and gross motor activities

Therapy Skill Builders
555 Academic Court
San Antonio, Texas 78204-2498

Tel (800) 228-0752
Fax (800) 232-1223

Toys and equipment for use in home and school, books and videotapes, assessment materials

Books

How Does Your Engine Run? A Leader's Guide to the Alert Program for Self-Regulation (M. Williams and S. Shellenberger, Therapy Works, 1994)

M.O.R.E. Integrating the Mouth with Sensory and Postural Functions, 2nd Edition (P. Oetter, E. Richter, S. Frick, PDP Press, 1995)

Making it Easy: Sensorimotor Activities at Home and School (M. Haldy and L Haack, Psychological Corporation, 1999)

Sensory Defensiveness in Children Aged 2-12: An Intervention Guide for Parents and Other Caretakers (P. Wilbarger and J. Wilbarger, Avanti Educational Programs PDP, 1991)

Sensory Integration and the Child (A. J. Ayres, Western Psychological Services, 1979)

*Sensory Integration: Theory and Practice** (A. Fisher, E. Murray, S. Lane, and A. Bundy, F. A. Davis Co., 2002)

Sensory Motor Handbook: A Guide for Implementing and Modifying Activities in the Classroom, 2nd Edition (J. Bissel, J. Fisher, C. Owens, and P. Polcyn, Therapy Skill Builders, 1998)

Sense-Abilities: Understanding Sensory Integration (M. Trott, M. Colby, M. Laurel, and S. Windeck, Communication Skill Builders, 1993)

*The Out-of-Sync Child: Recognizing and Coping with Sensory Integration Dysfunction** (C. Kranowitz, Perigee, 1998)

*The Out-of-Sync Child Has Fun: Activities for Kids with Sensory Integration Dysfunction** (C. Kranowitz, Perigee, 2003)

The Source for Autism (G. Richard, Linguisystems, 1997)

The Child with Special Needs: Encouraging Intellectual and Emotional Growth (S. Greenspan and S. Wieder, Perseus Publishing, 1998)

*Unlocking the Mysteries of Sensory Dysfunction** (E. Anderson and P. Emmons, Future Horizons Inc., 1996)

* These titles (and many others) are available online at www.SensoryResources.com.

Videos

Autism Insights. An interview with Temple Grandin and Lorna Jean King. A review of sensory defensiveness and positive effects of deep touch pressure. Available from Continuing Education Programs of America (309) 263-0310

Making Contact: Sensory Integration and Autism. Produced by Judith Reisman, Ph.D., OTR. A brief review of sensory integration theory and autism. Presents program offered at the Lorna Jean King's Center for Neurodevelopmental Studies, Available from Continuing Education Programs of America (309) 263-0310

The Out-of-Sync Child. *Featuring Carol Stock Kranowitz, M.A. Available from Sensory Resources (888) 357-5867

*Sensory Processing From Roots to Wings.** Prepared by Judith Reisman, Ph.D. Available through Pocket Full of Therapy (800) 736-8124

*Tools for Students.** Prepared by Diana Henry. Offers occupational therapy activity suggestions for home and school.

*Tools for Teachers.** Prepared by Diana Henry. Practical occupational therapy tips for teachers, both available through Henry OT (888) 371-1204 or www.henryot.com

Progressive Relaxation Training Tape. Prepared by Brian Doan, Ph.D. Available through Doan at (416) 483-4973

*These videos (and many others) are available online at www.SensoryResources.com.

Websites

Henry Occupational Therapy Services: www.henryot.com

Strategies for occupational therapists, teachers and parents

Marie's Sensory Integration Page: www.mindspring.com/~mariep/si/sensory.integration.html

A mother's web site reviewing sensory integration strategies

The Out-of-Sync Child: www.out-of-sync-child.com

This website has extensive links to information and products for children affected by sensory disorders. It includes more than a dozen pages of resources.

Sensory Resources: www.SensoryResources.com

Publishes books, music, CDs, audiotapes on sensory disorders. Also sponsors workshops to parents, teachers, and therapists. This website includes extensive links to other sensory resources.

Sensory Integration Resource Center: www.sinetwork.org

Link to the DSI parent connection and to the latest scientific research on sensory disorders and related topics.

Future Horizons: www.FutureHorizons-autism.com

World's largest publisher on autism, Asperger's Syndrome, and related topics.

References

Sensory Integration

Ackeman, D. (1991). *A Natural History of the Senses*. New York, NY: Vintage Books

Anderson, E. and Emmons, P. (1996), *Unlocking the Mysteries of Sensory Dysfunction* Arlington, Texas: Future Horizons, Inc.

Ayres, A. J. (1972). *Sensory Integration and Learning Disabilities*. Los Angeles: Western Psychological Services.

Ayres, A. J. (1972). *Southern California Sensory Integration Tests*. Los Angeles, California: Western Psychological Services.

Ayres, A. J. and Heskett, W. (1972). *Sensory integrative dysfunction in a young schizophrenic girl*. Journal of Autism and Childhood Schizophrenia, 2, 174-181,

Ayres, A. J. (1979) *Sensory Integration and the Child* Los Angeles Western Psychological Services.

Ayres, A. J. (1989) *Sensory Integration and Praxis Tests*. Los Angeles: Western Psychological Services.

Ayres, A. J. and Tickle, L. (1980). *Hyper-responsivity to touch and vestibular stimuli as a predictor of positive response EG sensory integration procedures by autistic children*. American Journal of Occupational Therapy 34, 375 381.

Ayres, A. J. and Mailloux, Z. (1983), *Possible pubertal effect on therapeutic gains in an autistic girl*. American Journal of Occupational Therapy 34, 375-381.

Baranek, G. and Berkson, G. (1994). Tactile defensiveness in children with developmental disabilities: responsiveness and habituatlon. Journal of Autism and Developmental Disorders Vol. 24, No. 4, 457-472.

Becker, M. (1980). Autism: a neurological model, AOTA Sensory Integration Special Interest Section Newsletter, 3 (1).

Berk, R. and DeGangi, G. (1983). DeGangi-Berk Test of Sensory Integration. Los Angeles: Western Psychological Services.

Bissell, J., Fisher, J., Owens, C., and Polcyn, P. (1988). Sensory Motor Handbook: A Guide for Implementing and Modifying Activities in the Classroom. Torrance, CA: Sensory Integration International.

Bloomer, M. and Rose, C. (1989). Frames of reference: guiding treatment for children with autism. Developmental Disabilities: A Handbook for Occupational Therapists. 12-26, The Haworth Press

Bonadonna, P. (1981). Effects of a vestibular stimulation program on stereotypic rocking behaviour. American Journal of Occupational Therapy, 35, 775-781.

Bright, T. and Bittick, L. (1981). Reduction of self-injurious behaviour using sensory integrative techniques. American Journal of Occupational. Therapy, 35, 167-173.

Chu, S. (1991). Sensory integration and autism: a review of the literature. Sensory Integration Quarterly, XIX, (3).

Cimorelli, J., Tilley, A, Wood, C. Highfill, M. (1996). The Effects of Sensory Integration Therapy on the Language skills of Children with Autism. ASA Conference Proceedings, Washington, DC: Autism Society 01 America.

Clark, F. (1983). Research on neuropathophysiology of autism and its implications for Occupational therapy. Occupational Therapy Journal of Research, 3, 3-22.

Cook, D. (1990). A sensory approach to the treatment and management of children with autism. Focus on Autistic Behaviour, 5 (6), 1-19.

Cool, S. (1990, Dec.). Use of a surgical brush in treatment of sensory defensiveness; Commentary and exploration. Sensory Integration Special Interest Newsletter. 4-6.

DeGangi, G. (1994). Documenting Sensorimotor Progress, San Antonio, Texas; Therapy Skill Builders.

Duker, P. and Rasing, E. (1989). Effects of redesigning the physical environment on self-stimulation and on-task behaviour in three autistic-type developmentally disabled individuals. Journal of Autism and Developmental Disorders, 19, 449-461.

Dunn, W. and Fisher, J. (1993). Sensory Registration, Autism and Tactile Defensiveness. Sensory Integration Special Interest Section Newsletter. 6 (2), 3-4.

Dunn, W. and Westman, K. (1996). The Sensory Profile: The performance of a national sample of children without disabilities. American Journal of Occupational Therapy, 51 (1)

Durand, D. and Crimmins, D. (1992). Motivation Assessment Scale. Topeka, Kansas; Monaco and Associates.

Edelson, S. (1984). Implications of sensory stimulation in self-destructive behaviour. American Journal of Mental Deficiency.

Fink, B. (1990). Sensory-Motor Integration Activities. Tuscon, Arizona: Therapy Skill Builders.

Fisher, A, Murray, E., and Bundy, A. (1991). Sensory Integration Theory and Practice, Philadelphia; F. A. Davis Company.

Frick, S. (1989, June). Sensory defensiveness: A case study. Sensory Integration Special Interest Section Newsletter, 4-6.

Grandin, T. (1992). Calming effects of deep touch pressure in patients with autistic disorder, college students, and animals. Journal of Child and Adolescent Psychopharmacology, 2 (1), 63-72,

Haldy, M. and Haack, L. (1995). Making It Easy: Sensorimotor activities at Home and. School Tucson, Arizona; Therapy Skill Builders.

Huebner, R. (1992). Autistic disorder; A neuropsychological enigma. American Journal of Occupational Therapy. 46, 487-501.

Inamura, K. N., Wiss, T., and Parham, D. (1990). The effects of hug machine usage on the behavioural organization of children with autism and autistic-like characteristics. Part I. Sensory Integration Quarterly, XVII.

Inamura, K. N., Wiss, T., and Parham, D. (1990). The effects of hug machine usage on the behavioural organization of children with autism and autistic-like characteristics. Part 2. Sensory Integration Quarterly, XVIII.

Iwasaki, K. and Holm, M. (1989). Sensory Treatment for the reduction of stereotypic behaviours in person with severe multiple disabilities. Occupational Therapy Journal Of Research, 9, 170-183.

Johnson, H. and Scott, A (1993). A Practical Approach to Saliva Control. San Antonio, Texas; Communication Skill Builders.

Kientz, M. and Dunn, W. (1997). A comparison of the performance of children with and without autism on the sensory profile. American Journal of Occupational Therapy, 51.(7), 530-537.

King, L. J. (1987). A sensory-integrative approach to the education of the autistic child. Sensory Integrative Approaches in Occupational Therapy. The Hawthorne Press, 77-85.

King, L. J. (1991). Sensory integration: an effective approach to therapy and education. Autism Research Review International. 5, 2.

Knickerbocker, B. (1980) A Holistic Approach to Treatment of Learning Disorders. Thorofare, New Jersey: Charles B. Slack.

Kranowitz, C. (1998) The Out of Sync Child. New York: Skylight Press Books.

Krauss, K. (1987). The effects of deep-pressure touch on anxiety. American Journal of Occupational Therapy 41, 366-73.

Larrington, G. (1987). A sensory integration based program with a severely retarded/autistic teenager; an occupational therapy case report. In: Mailloux, Z. (ed) Sensory Integrative Approaches in Occupational Therapy. New York: The Haworth Press.

Marshall, V. (1997). Drooling: Guidelines and Activities. Temecula, Calif.: Speech Dynamics Inc.

Miller. L. J. and Mcintosh, N. (1998). The diagnosis, treatment, and etiology of sensory modulation disorder. Sensory Integration Special Interest Section Quarterly, 21 (1).

Mora, J. and Kashman N. (1997). Teaming and the use of sensory integration strategies in early intervention. The Morning News.

Morris, S. and Klein, M. (1987). Pre-feeding Skills. Tucson, Arizona: Therapy Skill Builders.

Morton, K. and Wolford, M. (1994). Analysis of Sensory Behaviour Inventory. Arcadia, CA: Skills with Occupational Therapy.

Nelson, D., Nitzberg, L., and Hollander, T. (1980). Visually monitored postrotary nystagmus in seven autistic children. American Journal of Occupational Therapy. 34, 382-386.

Oetter, P., Richter, E., and Frick, S. (1988). M.O.R.E.: Integrating the Mouth with Sensory And Postural Functions. Hugo, MN: PDP Press.

Ornitz, E. M. and Ritvo, E. R. (1968). Perceptual constancy in early infantile autism. Archives of General Psychiatry, 28, 76-98.

Ornitz, E. M. et al. (1969). Decreased postrotary nystagmus in early infantile autism. Neurology, 19, 653-658.

Ornitz, E. M. (1970). Vestibular Dysfunction in schizophrenia and childhood autism. Comprehensive Psychiatry.

Ornitz, E. M. (1973). The modulation of sensory input and motor output in autistic children. In: Schopler, E. and Reichler, (eds.) Psychopathology and Child Development. New York: Plenum.

Ornitz, E. M. (1985). Neurophysiology of infantile autism. Journal of the American Academy of of Child Psychiatry, 24 251-262.

Ornitz, E. M., Lane, S., Suigiyama, T., de Traversay, J. (1993). Startle modulation studies in autism. Journal of Autism and Developmental Disorders, Vol. 23, No. 4, 619-637.

Peterson, T. (1986). Recent studies in autism: a review of the literature. Occupational Therapy in Mental Health, 6 63-75.

Pettit, K. (1980). Treatment of the autistic child: A demanding challenge. Sensory Integration Special Interest Section Newsletter, 3- 4.

Reilly, C., Nelson, D., and Bundy, A. (1983). Sensorimotor versus fine motor activities in eliciting vocalizations in autistic children. Occupational Therapy Journal of Research, 3, 199-212.

Reisman, J. and Hanschu B. (1992). Sensory Integration Inventory-Revised for Individuals with Developmental Disabilities: User's Guide, Hugo, MN: PDP Press.

Reisman, J. and Gross, A (1992). Psychophysiological measurement of treatment effects in an adult with sensory defensiveness. Canadian Journal of Occupational Therapy, 59 (5), 248-257

Reisman, J. (1993) Using a sensory integrative approach to treat self-Injurious behaviour in an adult with profound mental retardation. American Journal of Occupational Therapy, 47 (5) 403-411.

Royeen, C. (1986), The development of a touch scale for measuring tactile defensiveness in children American Journal of Occupational Therapy, 40, 414-418.

Sutton, S. (1997). My Big Ball Book. Collingwood, Ont: Occupational Therapy for Children.

Sutton, S. (1997). My Exercise Book, Collingwood, Ont: Occupational Therapy for Children.

Sutton, S, (1997). My Scooter Board Book. Collingwood, Ont: Occupational Therapy for Children.

Sensory Integration International (1991). A Parents' Guide to Understanding Sensory Integration. Torrance, CA: Sensory Integration International Inc.

Slavik, B. A. and Ayres, A. J. (1984). Vestibular stimulation and eye contact in autistic children. Neuropaediatrics, 15, 33-36.

Trott, M., Laurel, M., and Windeck, S. (1993). Sense-Abilities: Understanding Sensory Integration. Tucson, Arizona: Therapy Skill Builders.

Wilbarger, P. (1984). Planning and adequate sensory diet: Application of sensory processing theory during the first year of life. Zero to Three, Vol. 10, 7-12.

Wilbarger, P. and Wilbarger, J. (1991). Sensory Defensiveness in Children ages 1-12: An Intervention Guide for Parents and Other Caretakers. Santa Barbara California: Avanti Educational Programs.

Wilbarger, P. (1995). The Sensory Diet: Activity programs based on sensory processing theory. Sensory Integration Special Interest Section Newsletter 18, 2.

Williams. M. and Shellenberger, S. (1994). How Does your Engine Run? The Alert Program For Self-Regulation. Albuquerque, New Mexico: Therapy Works,

Willlamson, G. and Anzalone, M. (1996). Sensory Integration: a key component of the evaluation and treatment of young children with severe difficulties in relating and communicating. Assessing and Treating Infants and Young Children with Severe Difficulties in Relating and Communicating. Arlington, VA: Zero to Three, 29-36.

Windeck, S. and Laurel, M. (1989). A theoretical framework combining speech-language therapy with sensory integration. Sensory Integration Special Interest Newsletter, 11.

Wiss, T. (1987). Literature review: visuo-vestibular stimulation as related to visual attention in the autistic child. AOTA Developmental Disabilities Special Interest Section Newsletter, 10.

Wblkowicz, R., Fish, J., and Schaffer, R. (1977). Sensory integration with autistic children. Canadian Journal of Occupational Therapy, 44, 171-176.

Yack, E. (1997) Sensory integration and children with pervasive developmental disorders. IMPrint, Vol. 18.

Zissermann, L. (1992). The effects of deep pressure on self-stimulating behaviours in a child with autism and other disabilities. American Journal of Occupational Therapy, 46, 547-551.

Pervasive Developmental Disorders

Adams, J. (1993). Autism-PDD: Creative Ideas During the School Years. Kent Bridge, Ont: Adams Publications.

Adams, J. (1997). Autism-PDD: More Creative Ideas From Age Eight to Early Adulthood. Kent Bridge, Ont: Adams Publications.

American Psychiatric Association (1994). Diagnostic and Statistical Manual of Mental Disorders. 4th Ed Washington DC: American Psychiatric Association.

Attwood, A. (1993). Movement disorders and autism: a rationale for the use of Facilitated communication and an alternative model for training staff and students. In 1993 International Conference Proceedings: Autism A World of Options. International Conference on Autism, Toronto. Arlington, Texas: Future Education.

Baron Cohen, S. (1994). Mindblindness: an Essay on Autism and Theories of Mind. Cambridge, Mass: MIT Press.

Bettlelheim, B. (1967). The Empty Fortress. New York: Free Press.

Bauman, M. and Kemper, T. (1994). Neurobiology of Autism. Baltimore: Johns Hopkins.

Delacoto, C. (1974). The Ultimate Stranger. Doubleday Books.

Doan, B. (1994). Brief Relaxation Exercises. Geneva Centre Course Materials.

Donnellan, A. and Leary, M. (1995) Movement and Diversify in Autism/Mental Retardation. Madison, Wis: DRI Press.

Freedman, S. and Dake, L. (1996), Teach Me Language. Langley, BC: KF Books.

Frith, U. (1989). Autism: Explaining the Enigma. Oxford, England: Blackwell.

Frost, L. and Bondy, A. (1994). The Picture Exchange Communication System Training Manual, Cherry Hill, NJ; PECs Inc.

Gray, C. (1993). The Social Story Book. Jenison, MI: Jenison Public Schools.

Greenspan, S. (1992). Reconsidering the diagnosis and treatment of very young children with autistic spectrum or pervasive developmental disorder. Zero to Three, 13, 1-9-

Greenspan, S. and Wieder, S. (1998). The Child with Special Needs: Encouraging Intellectual and Emotional Growth. Reading, Mass: Addison-Wesley.

Groden, J., Cautela, J., Prince, S., and Berryman, J. (1994). The impact of stress and anxiety on individuals with autism and developmental disabilities. In Behavioural

Issues in Autism, edited by E. Schopler and G. Mesibov, 177-194, New York: Plenum Press.

Groden, J. and LeVasseur, P. (1995). Cognitive picture rehearsal: A visual system to teach self-control. In Teaching Children with Autism: Methods to Enhance Learning, Communication, and Socialization. edited by K. Quill. Albany, New York: Delmar Publishing Co.

Hill, D. and Leary, M. (1993). Movement Disturbance: A Clue to Hidden Competencies in Persons Diagnosed with Autism and Other Developmental Disabilities. Madison, Wis: DRI Press.

Hodgdon, L. (1995). Visual Strategies for Improving Communication. Troy, Michigan; Quirk Roberts Publishing.

Irlen, H. (1991). Reading by the Colours. Overcoming Dyslexia and other Reading Disabilities Through the Irlen Method. New York:

Avery Publishing Group Inc.

Janzen, J. (1996). Understanding the Nature of Autism, San Antonio, Texas: Therapy Skill Builders.

Kanner, L. (1943). Autistic disturbances of affective contact. Nervous Child, 2, 217-250,

Kaplan, M. (1992). Visual therapy and autism. The Facilitator, 2, 2.

Lovaas, 0. (1981). Teaching Developmentally Disabled Children: The Me Book. Baltimore, MD: University Park Press.

Madel, J. and Rose, D. (1994). Auditory Integration Training. American Journal of Audiology, 3, 1, 14-18.

Maurice, C. (1996). Behavioural Intervention for Young Children with Autism. Austin, Texas: Pro-Ed.

Miller, A. and Miller, E. (1989). From Ritual to Repertoire: A Cognitive-Developmental Systems Approach with Behaviour-Disordered. Children, New York: John Wiley and Sons.

Quill, K. (Ed. 1995). Teaching Children with Autism: Strategies to Enhance Communication and Socialisation. Albany, New York;

Delmar Publishers.

Quill, K. (1995). Visually cued instruction for children with autism and pervasive developmental disorders. Focus on Autistic Behaviour, 10, 10-20.

Richard, G. (1997). The Source for Autism. East Moline, Illinois Linguisystems.

Siegel, B. (1996). The World of the Autistic Child. New York: Oxford University Press.

Williams, D. (1996). Autism-An Inside-Out Approach. England; Cromwell Press.

First Hand Accounts

Barron, J. and Barron, S. (1992). There's a Boy In Here. New York: Simon and Schuster.

Cesaroni, L. and Garbcr, M. (1991). Exploring the experience of autism through firsthand accounts. Journal of Autism and Developmental Disorders, 21, 303-313.

Grandin, T. (1984). My experiences as an autistic child and review of selected literature. Journal of Orthomolecular Psychiatry, 13, 144-174.

Grandin, T. and Scariano. (1986). Emergence: Labeled Autistic. Novato, California. Arena Press.

Grandin, T, (1995) Thinking in Pictures and Other Reports from My Life With Autism. New York: Doubleday Inc.

McKean, T. (1994). Soon Will Come the Light Arlington, Texas: Future Horizons, Inc.

SteIhi, A. (1991). The Sound of a Miracle A Child's Triumph Over Autism. New York: Doubleday Inc. York: John Wiley and Sons.

Williams D. (1992). Nobody Nowhere. New York: Times Books.

Williams, D. (1994), Somebody Somewhere, New York: Times Books

Index

A

Assessment   15, 17-19, 38, 54, 70, 187-188, 192

Autism   3, 7, 9, 11-13, 17, 23, 27, 33, 38-39, 54, 70-72, 107, 179, 186, 189, 191-198

Ayres, Jean, Ph. D., OTR   7, 12-13, 17, 22, 24, 35, 37-39, 45, 144, 189, 191, 195

B

Balloon, fidget toy   179, 181

Blowing   78, 85-86, 103-104, 130, 134-135, 142

Bungee cord bracelet   80, 179, 183

C

Calming techniques   77, 125

Challenging behaviours   14, 53, 69, 73

Checklist   5, 39, 57, 59, 61, 63, 65, 67

Chewing   49, 61-63, 78-79, 84, 104, 133, 135

Childcare   6-7, 9, 15, 107, 110-111, 123, 179

Childcare settings   6, 107, 110-111

Chin; keeping dry   50, 61, 127, 135-137

Circle time   15, 29, 50, 63, 76

Communication   6, 11-12, 19-20, 31, 36-38, 86, 97-98, 105, 109-112, 119-120, 122-124, 143-144, 189, 193, 196-197

D

Defensiveness   5, 25-26, 30, 69-72, 78-84, 96-97, 99, 101-102, 104, 109, 116-117, 119, 125, 129, 137, 189, 191-192, 194-195

Dressing   5-6, 16-18, 33, 42, 59-60, 97-98

Dressing checklist   5, 59

Drinking   61, 101, 109

Dyspraxia   32

E

Eating   5-6, 16, 37, 42-43, 61-62, 72, 82, 102-103, 116, 138

Eating checklist   5, 61

Notes and Ideas to Try

Notes and Ideas to Try

Notes and Ideas to Try

2200 E. Patrick Lane, Suite 3A
Las Vegas, NV 89119
Tel. 888-357-5867
Fax: 702-891-8899
email: Orders@SensoryResources.com
www.SensoryResources.com